LEGENDS, LORE
〄・AND SECRETS OF ・〄
NEW ENGLAND

THOMAS D'AGOSTINO AND ARLENE NICHOLSON

THE
History
PRESS

Published by The History Press
Charleston, SC 29403
www.historypress.net

Copyright © 2013 by Thomas D'Agostino and Arlene Nicholson
All rights reserved

Front bottom cover photo by Eric Charles Steinhart.

Photos by Arlene Nicholson unless otherwise noted.

First published 2013

Manufactured in the United States

ISBN 978.1.60949.946.4

Library of Congress CIP data applied for.

This book is dedicated to all.
You never know who will become a legend for future generations to admire.

Contents

Contents

ACKNOWLEDGEMENTS

As usual, there are so many people who have made this book possible. We are grateful to all for your assistance and expertise. Grateful thanks and praise go out to the Burrillville Historical Society; Rutland Historical Society; *Sam's Good News* in Rutland; Putnam Public Library; Greenville Public Library; Foster Town Hall; Scituate Town Hall; everyone at the Kennebunk Inn; Ron Kolek; Ron Kolek Jr.; Christopher Balzano and Massachusetts Crossroads; Matthew Moniz of Spooky South Coast; Brian Harnois; Jason Mayoh; Christian White; Kent Spottswood; Sheila and Beth Williams; Skip Gervais at the Mill in Greenville; the good people of Portsmouth, New Hampshire; Jeff Saraceno; Carl Johnson; Blackstone Valley Tourism Council / Tour Southern New England; Tom and Sue Wood; Greg and Magin Wood; Patti Roden; Kevin Fay; High Life Ski Lodge; Hampton Historical Society; Princeton Historical Society; Mulligan's in Biddeford; Mandy Pincins; Webster Library; the *Patriot* newspaper; the *Yankee Shopper*; Tavern on Main; Smith's Castle; Barbara Thaeder; and all those who wished to remain anonymous but were vital in the making of this book.

Introduction

New England is a magical land where the boundaries of time and timelessness create a seam of our existence that is often stranger than fiction. The antiquity of the region is ripe for legends and stories that, if not for documentation, would certainly be thought the work of some far-out writer or storyteller. Within the pages of this book are the legends and the actual facts that somehow took a back burner to more potent storylines that would become the accepted views of what transpired. Lucy Keyes, Hannah Frank, John Burke, Hannah Robinson, William Blackstone and many more hold special places in our history and should be addressed with as much accuracy as time and archaic writings will allow. This also goes for the places that have made New England a special region worth exploring.

The characters and places you are about to acquaint yourself with may seem too far-fetched to be true in some cases, but be assured that these pieces of history have much more than a thread of truth running through them. In some cases, you will read anecdotes of historical phrases or terms that have either passed from generation to generation without the knowledge of their origin or have been modified and twisted into slang to fit the day. In other cases, there is much more behind some of the timeworn legends we have come to accept.

This compendium has no time frame. It covers some of our favorite events, places and people throughout the region. These accounts have a beginning, and at some point in time, someone was the first to pen them for history's sake. Painstaking efforts to find those first writings have resulted in more than their share of conflicting accounts for some of the legends within this book. Others have been compiled from several sources to be collected into a single work for the first time. Some of these stories of legends and lore are hundreds of years old, while others have yet to become perennial tales to be told on cold nights when the New England wind whistles about the windows and the shadows grow long with the ever-dimming light.

LUCY KEYES

The Lost Child of Wachusett

As the sun begins to descend within the shadow of Wachusett Mountain, a voice is heard echoing in the wind. Rather soft at first, the reverberations grow louder with each beckoning until the now attentive listener can easily recognize the moan, "Lucy! Luuucyyyy!"

It is not the scream of a banshee but rather a mother's desperate plea for one little girl to come home, a little girl who has been lost for centuries. Her mother, Martha Keyes, has also long passed and is but dust in the grave. Yet her spirit roams in the twilight hours, eternally searching for her lost daughter, four-year-old Lucy Keyes, who disappeared more than two and a half centuries ago.

Robert Keyes (September 21, 1711–March 1, 1795) married Martha Bowker on December 24, 1740. Together, they had ten children. In 1751, Robert and Martha Keyes bought two hundred acres of land from Benjamin Muzzey and settled on the southeastern slope of Wachusett Mountain in Princeton, Massachusetts. Princeton was incorporated in 1759, so the land was sparsely settled; their closest neighbor, legend says, was a recluse named Tilly Littlejohn.

Shortly after moving to Princeton, Martha gave birth to Lucy. The little girl had the eyes of her father and the beauty of her mother. On April 14, 1755, Martha sent her two older daughters—Patty, age seven, and Anna, age nine—to Wachusett Pond to fetch some white sand for the purpose of making a polishing agent for their pewter. It was common practice to also spread the sand on the floor around the stove or working area to soak up any grease or fat from the meat while it was being prepared. It also served to keep any embers or stray sparks from igniting the wooden floors. Lucy somehow managed to follow her sisters to the lake, where they immediately told her to turn around and get home or mother would be very upset.

Before long, the two girls returned from their task and inquired as to Lucy's whereabouts. Being so preoccupied with her chores, the mother had not seen Lucy slip away out the door and down the trail toward the pond with the two girls. Little Lucy apparently never made it back to the home.

Martha rushed frantically out into the wild of the mountain, screaming Lucy's name. Some folks nearby heard the clamor and summoned Robert Keyes, who quickly formed a search party in the hopes of finding the young girl as the day slivered its last shards of light over the countryside. The only evidence attesting to where Lucy may have wandered were a few broken twigs at the end of the trail.

For several days, neighbors searched the mountainside for Lucy, but to no avail. Those who helped in the search felt despair for Robert and Martha Keyes, and those who lived in the distance heard, for days, one desperate cry echo over the mountain: "Lucy! Luuuucyyy!"

In time, the search was called off, for it was certain that Indians or one of the wild animals of the mountain had taken young Lucy. Robert Keyes inquired with the nearby tribes as to any sign they may have seen of his daughter, but none had seen hide or hair of her. Martha, in what some claim was despondency and others madness, continued to roam the woods every night, calling Lucy's name in the hopes that her little girl might return to her. For the next thirty-one years, her voice would resonate through the hillside calling for her lost child.

When Martha died on August 9, 1789, at the age of sixty-eight, the neighbors, although saddened by her passing, were relieved that the mountain would no longer resound with the eerie ranting of Mrs. Keyes' pleas for her daughter to come home. Shortly after Martha was laid to eternal repose, the residents around the Keyes homestead were tossed from their slumber by an unnerving wail echoing over the hillside. It was the voice of Martha Keyes calling, "Lucy! Luuuucyyy!"

At this point, the telling of this account comes to a fork in the road of legend and lore. The most accepted version of the tale recounts that several years after the deaths of both Martha and Robert Keyes, a letter was found written by their recluse neighbor, Tilly Littlejohn, describing what happened to young Lucy Keyes on that fateful day back in 1755. Littlejohn admitted on his deathbed that he came across Lucy while strolling in the woods and killed her by repeatedly slamming her body against a log. He then stuffed her body in a hollow log and waited until nightfall to return and bury her under an uprooted tree.

His reason for the dastardly deed was that he had always blamed Robert Keyes for stealing a portion of his land. When the matter was taken to court, the judge found in favor of Keyes and thus granted the land to Robert and his family. From that day on, Littlejohn vowed a secret revenge on the people who he was certain had stolen his land. When he saw young Lucy, her eyes reminded him of her father's and how they stared straight back at him in court not long ago when he stated quite frankly that the land was purchased fair and square. Littlejohn lost his temper, and before he realized what he had done, little Lucy lay dead in the snow. He even joined in on the search for the girl as not to arouse suspicion. When he realized that the hunt for the girl was not going to wane in a hurry, he stole away under the cloak of darkness and removed the body to a better hiding place.

There are historians who believe that Littlejohn had nothing to do with the disappearance of Lucy and that she may have been taken by some wild beast or wandering band of Indians. There are several facts that support this claim. The letter surfaced in about 1827. Tilly Littlejohn was born on May 26, 1735, and died on November 1, 1793, in nearby Sterling from consumption. He never lived next to Robert Keyes in 1755. In fact, at the time Lucy disappeared, he was not old enough to own land. The closest neighbor to the Keyes family in 1755 was Benjamin Houghton, who owned the land bounding the Keyes place. Only the west side, owned by the province, was not Houghton's. There was never any known quarrel over the land.

On April 23, 1755, Young Littlejohn joined Captain Asa Whitcomb's company in the Battle of Crown Point. He was discharged in October of that year. He married Hannah Brooks of Lancaster in December 1757, and they had six children, two of whom survived to maturity. When he passed, Hannah and his son John and daughter Pamela acquired his estate, including the acreage he purchased from Keyes in 1759. So, if records serve correctly, Littlejohn was not a recluse nor did he even live near the Keyes family at the time of Lucy's disappearance.

At one point, Robert Keyes, financially strained from his constant travels in search of his lost daughter, petitioned the General Court of Massachusetts for some sort of financial relief. Every bit of news that a young child was in the company of an Indian camp brought him hope and set him in search of that camp. With no finances left, he had no choice but to sell portions of his land, starting in 1759. By 1773, he had but fifty acres of his original two hundred retained for his own living purposes.

Years after Lucy's disappearance, a party of fur trappers returning from northern Vermont mentioned meeting a "White Squaw" in an Indian camp. Her only English was mostly unintelligible gibbering, but the word "Wachusett" was contained in her phrases. When the fur trappers surmised that it could have been the long-lost Lucy Keyes, they inquired if she would like to go to Wachusett with them but were informed that she was happily married and refused to leave the camp. Either way, Martha Keyes, never knowing the fate of her lost daughter, still haunts the mountainside, desperately calling for the little girl's return.

Lucy is also thought to haunt the hills as well. Witnesses have seen the glimmering figure of a little girl wandering aimlessly in the woods around the mountain. Wachusett offers nighttime skiing at the mountain, where the trails are well lit and accommodating for those who are the nocturnal sort. Skiers and snow groomers have heard the reverberations of Martha's ghostly voice chanting over the mountain. Some claim to have seen small footprints in the freshly fallen or groomed snow resembling those of a child. These little barefoot indentations in the white powder could only indicate one thing: Lucy is still searching for the way home.

I have had the pleasure of skiing the trails of Wachusett Mountain, but unfortunately, I have never heard the voice of Martha Keyes or spied the visage of Lucy searching for her home. I was too busy tumbling head over heels down the slopes much of the time.

If you do not have the opportunity to roam Wachusett Mountain in the hopes of getting a glimpse of Lucy Keyes or her mother, you can visit the Princeton Historical Society, where you may behold the actual cradle in which Lucy Keyes once slept.

WHICH ROCK IS WITCH ROCK?

Most people do not believe in witches today, at least not the way they did centuries ago. Religious folk dreaded the very whisper of the word, and those who were thought to be in league with the devil were either outcast to begin with or banished from towns and settlements, left to find refuge in the outskirts of communities. Legends abound of these "hags" who instigated fear in the hearts of the pious. Many have left their names and stories in tomes to be recounted throughout the eras, but in Foster, Rhode Island, a boulder stands as a monument of testimony to the local life of one particular witch.

Nestled in the woods near what was once Hopkins Hill, a specific boulder that is notched with a peculiar mark is now known as Witch Rock. The rock came to gain its name and reputation more than two centuries ago when an old hag named Pat Jenkins came to settle in a deserted cabin within eyeshot of the glacial refuse. The locals said that her presence gave the woods an ominous, foreboding ambiance that repelled all who sought to enter the cursed domain. It was rumored that she accomplished this by putting an evil spell on the perimeter of the land she called home. Hideous figures were often seen flitting about among the trees and shrubs of the blighted real estate. Her powers of darkness reached beyond her boundaries to the neighbors' homes, where tools and other such homesteading items would disappear without a trace. Cattle became afflicted with disease, and stones flew out of nowhere, hitting homes and breaking windows. Of course, all of these occurrences were instantly blamed on Pat Jenkins, solidifying that she was in league with the dark one.

During stormy weather, the old witch could be seen rising from the thicket, stirring the clouds and moving them at will to her desired position over the land. Neighboring crops fell victim to hail, frost and other unfathomable horrors at the swish of her enchanted broom. It is legend to this day that for one hundred yards surrounding the rock, the ground is cursed and must never be disturbed lest the trespasser of the evil circle will fall prey to calamity.

A long time ago, a local farmer named Reynolds decided that the curse was a bunch of bunk and vowed that he would break the enchanted parcel of earth with his team and plough, thus proving the legend to be no more than an old wives' tale. His neighbors, though leery of his ridicule, decided to watch from a distance to see if the man would successfully defy the witch's curse.

The team began to pull the plough through the rocky terrain with little incident until it reached the inner boundary of the magic circle. At that moment, the plow veered as if invisible hands had taken control of its course, and the landside—or chip, as it was known—became dislodged from the digging implement. Mr. Reynolds, undaunted by this incident, replaced the chip, and the team started once more.

With the speed and tenacity only a witch could conjure, the oxen became unyoked and the chip literally "jumped" from the plough and reeled through the air out of sight. This bizarre happening caused the onlookers to reconsider their position and retreat closer to their homes. All at once, there came from the north a large crow exhibiting curious behavior. The omen of evil landed on the gnarly branch of a dead tree and commenced cawing at the farmer. John Hopkins, owner of the land, shouted at the bird, "Squawk, you damned old Pat Jenkins!"

The crow took flight, dropping the chip at Reynolds's feet while also taking the form of an old woman with a cocked, pointed black hat. The hag furiously descended on the rock, but before the men could reach her, she transformed into a large black cat and sprang off into the woods, disappearing into the ground. The men commenced digging for the familiar yet found no trace of the minion of the devil. During the frenzy, one of the searchers, while digging for the witch's familiar, struck the blade of the shovel against the boulder with such intensity that it made a furrow in the precipice.

After that wicked incident, few dared to enter the haunted woods where the witch's cabin stood. The ruins of a small dwelling sit to this day near a giant rock formation 564 feet above sea level on what is now known as Witch Hill, and the furrow is hidden in the moss and lichen that grows from the rock that Pat Jenkins claimed as her own centuries ago.

Rock atop Witch Hill in Foster, where no man has dared to plant crops. It remains a wooded area to this day. Notice the chip taken from the stone.

There is another such formation known as Witch Rock in Rochester, Massachusetts. The rock is adorned with the silhouette of a witch wearing a tall, wide-brimmed hat and flying on a broom. Under the figure are the words "Witch Rock," painted in bold black letters. The rock is tucked under some trees, on the north side of New Bedford Road just as it intersects Vaughan Hill Road. It is located on private property but can be easily viewed from the road.

The legend of this rock hails back to when Europeans first arrived in the New World. The Sippican Indians believed that evil spirits would rise out from the large split in the rock and wreak havoc on them; therefore, they avoided meeting or stopping at that spot. The colonists, being fearful of witches and sorcery, believed that witches would rise from the rock on the nights of the full moon. There is another story of a woman being murdered at the rock. A woman accused of witchcraft fled Salem during the witch trials. When she got to the rock, her captors overtook her and killed her on the very spot.

The original idea to paint the witch on the face of the boulder came from Shirley Thompson in the 1950s. Thompson was a talented artist who had heard the many legends associated with the rock and decided to give it a proper moniker and logo. Her home, known as the Thompson Home to locals, was once called Witch Cottage. It has since become a landmark, serving as a guidepost for travelers along the New Bedford Road. There are more such landmarks in New England. They were believed to be evil omens just because they appeared to be out of the ordinary or in a strange setting. Such relics truly shed light on how the Indians and the early colonists feared the dark side.

William Blackstone

The title of this strange but true tale could be "Who Has the Box of Bones Containing William Blackstone?" or "Who Lost the Remains of the First Settler of Rhode Island?" This question of Rhode Island history poses an enigma. If you visit the town of Cumberland, Rhode Island, you will see a community rich with the history of industry and economical growth. Its mill houses and factory buildings, including the old Ann & Hope Mill Outlet, grace this parcel of land. It is an area abundant with stories and legends that are common of early America. But there is one story that takes the brass ring, and the extraordinary fact is that it is actually true.

If you visit the village of Lonsdale, a section of Cumberland, take a trip to the Ann & Hope Mill Outlet. It was once the largest mill outlet store in the state, and it is a monument to history in itself. Most of the store now stands vacant aside from the entities of the past that may still roam within its walls. There is still a small section where one may shop for weekly specials in gardening or other seasonal commodities. The building also houses a large flea market on the weekends.

After you have shopped to your desire, take a walk north of the parking lot, and you will see a monument in a small park. This monument is reported to be the final resting place of Rhode Island's first white settler, Reverend William Blackstone. There is one small problem, however: he is not resting there. Where is he then? Well, that is what many would like to know. His story after his death is more interesting and mysterious than his achievements of being first founder of Rhode Island and Boston, Massachusetts, and a minister of the Anglican Church. Let's start at the beginning, and maybe you as the reader can shed some light on this dilemma.

Reverend William Blackstone was twenty-eight years old when he came to the New World in 1623 as a part of the Robert Gorges expedition. Gorges and his throng settled in what is now Boston, Massachusetts, with the hopes of establishing an Episcopal colony. The colony did not last long, as the people grew tired of the savage wilderness and returned to more civil surroundings, namely England. Reverend Blackstone was a recluse by nature. His desire to stay clear of his fellow man led him to set up camp and live a solitary life, thus becoming the founder of that now great eastern city once called Shawmut. He was left with ample supplies and cattle. Blackstone pastured his livestock on a forty-six-acre cleared lot that would later be known as the Boston Common. Cattle grazed on the common well into the 1800s. The "Solitary of Shawmut," as Samuel Adams Drake called him, befriended the local Indians and lived in harmony with them for several years until the next wave of settlers came along.

John Winthrop and his Puritan brigade decided that Shawmut would make a great place to settle and teach their religious doctrine. Blackstone was not fond of their intrusion into his privacy. In fact, Blackstone, although reluctant at first, actually aided the settlers when sickness and starvation began to take its toll on them. An excerpt from Katherine Abbott's *Old Paths and Legends of New England* sums it up best:

> *In the summer of 1630, when the worthies Governor Winthrop, Coddington, and other men of Lincolnshire came to the Charles River from Salem, which pleased them not as a site for the capital, William Blaxton the recluse stepped forth from his solitary hut on his exclusive peninsula of Shawmut and offered them the hospitality of his spring and a share in his pasture on Boston Common. Whether he offered them "Blackstone apples" is not recorded, but this "man of a particular humour," soon wearied of the Lords-Brethren, as he had of the Lords-Bishops of England, and drove his cattle to far-distant Rehoboth.*

Present-day Cumberland was once part of the Rehoboth colony. The pronunciation and spelling of "Blaxton" has also changed over time to Blackstone.

Over the next few years, the two coexisted in reserved harmony. Reverend Blackstone soon reached his limits with the Puritan populace and sold his land (which is now Beacon Hill and Charles Street) to the

BLACKSTONE MONUMENT.

PUBLIC NOTICE.

JULY 4TH, 1856.

The members of the "BLACKSTONE MONUMENT ASSOCIATION," and all other Ladies and Gentlemen so disposed, are hereby notified and invited to assemble at the celebrated "CATHOLIC OAK," on the original homestead of the venerated Blackstone, near the Lonsdale Depot, on July 4th, at 10 o'clk., a.m.

☞ **Suitable and appropriate exercises may be expected.**

A beautiful model of the proposed Mausoleum in honor of CIVIL AND RELIGIOUS LIBERTY will be exhibited ; the

GREAT RECORD BOOK !

of the Association, exceeding in size and style all the books of the age, will be open to public inspection and for the reception of members. This is the first Anniversary of an Association which one year ago commenced with a single member and now numbers its members by thousands, and is destined to be the largest Association in the World.

☞ Refreshments will be provided, and Excursion Trains will run to and from the place.

BY ORDER OF THE PRESIDENT.

A. CRAWFORD GREENE & BROTHER, PRINTERS, Prov.

S. C. NEWMAN, Sec'y.

Flyer put out by the Blackstone Monument Association regarding the proposed monument that never materialized.

Puritans, who paid a sixpence each for the property. In May 1635, the good reverend headed south on the Pequot Trail toward present-day Rhode Island with his belongings—which included at one point the largest library in New England, numbering well over two hundred books and pamphlets—strapped to his cattle. Alongside him meandered his trusty tamed mouse-colored bull. He settled in present-day Cumberland. There he built a home removed from all other colonial influence and lived in his desired solitude consisting of himself, his livestock, his orchard and his library. He called his home Study Hill. Reverend Blackstone made friends with the local Indians and lived in harmony once more.

William Blackstone was not your usual colonial settler. While most walked or rode a horse, the reverend rode his trained and trusted bull. He is also credited with starting the first apple orchard in Rhode Island on this piece of real estate. His species of apples, called yellow sweeting, were said to be the tastiest fruit in the New World. Blackstone crossed and grafted other species to achieve this succulent delicacy. In *The History of Attleborough,* John Daggett noted that the species may have been created while Blackstone resided in Shawmut. As late as 1836, three of these trees still stretched toward the heavens in a meadow near Study Hill, two of which still bore the prized fruit for all to enjoy. Attempts have been made to graft the apples for historical and edible purposes.

Roger Williams, the founder of Providence and a man deserving of recognition for his achievements as well, ventured to this parcel of the Union in the year 1636 to stake his claim in history, one full year after William Blackstone came to forge the territory. The difference was that Roger Williams formed a colony, while William Blackstone remained a recluse. Blackstone and Williams became good friends, and the reverend ventured once a month from his home on Study Hill to Williams's trading post in Cocumcossuc in order to preach to the Indians at Roger Williams's request. The "Solitary of Shawmut" lived in peace among the local Indians in his self-imposed exile until 1659, when sixty-four-year-old William Blackstone wed Widow Sarah Stevenson of Boston, who brought with her an only child. His name was John. William and Sarah had one child together before she died in 1673, and the reverend followed two years later in 1675. He was eighty years old.

Shortly after, King Philip's War broke out among the colonists and Indians. The very natives he lived in harmony with burned his estate to the ground. As for William Blackstone, he was buried near his home on Study Hill, where his grave was marked by two boulders abreast a quartz stone marker. Buried next to him was his pet bull. It seemed that the reverend was soon forgotten as his property lay in ruins, a casualty of one of the bloodiest battles ever fought on American soil. John sold the property in 1692 and moved to Providence to make a living as a shoemaker.

It was not until 1855, 180 years later, that the life and death of William Blackstone was resurrected. At that time, a group of citizens gathered around the roughshod grave to pay tribute to their founder and raise money to have a proper, more modern monument erected in the place of the antiquated rock pile. Donations were taken, but the monument never materialized—and neither did any refunds.

More years would pass as time took its toll, and the weeds grew high, hiding William Blackstone's grave from common sight until the Lonsdale Company, owned by the firm of Brown and Ives, decided to expand its operations by building a mill on the Blackstone River. This meant leveling Study Hill and moving Reverend Blackstone's remains to another place. Luckily, a certain William Gammell was not only one of the directors of the Lonsdale Company but also the president of the Rhode Island Historical Society. So, when the Ann & Hope Mill was to take the place of Study Hill, Gammell saved the remains of William Blackstone from being exhumed and lost—at least, for a while.

A special meeting was held on July 26, 1886, where it was written that on May 6, 1886, Providence undertakers Miles and Luther had exhumed the grave of William Blackstone only to find a few pieces of bone, some bone dust and the remaining nails that once held together his long since deteriorated coffin. These artifacts were put in a special lead-sealed box and were prepared for reburial. Witnesses to this historic act were Mr. Gammell himself and an ancestor of Reverend Blackstone, Mr. Lorenzo Blackstone. An excerpt from the 1885 state census of Rhode Island noted, "Study Hill, the site of William Blackstone's residence from 1635 till his death 1675, and also the site of his burial. His remains were disinterred May 6, 1886, 211 years, lacking 20 days, after his death. A monument will mark their future resting place."

Three years later, the company decided that it was going to erect a monument in honor of the great reverend. At another meeting, held on July 26, 1889, the descendants of Mr. Blackstone resolved to bear the expenses of erecting the monument, as it would relate the history, in their words (as accurately as possible), of the life and attributes of William Blackstone. The Lonsdale Company had no objections. Now is where things begin to get sketchy and plans went awry.

According to Amelia Daggert Sheffield, who had taken her father's accounts and edited them for the book *A Sketch of the History of Attleborough From Its Settlement to the Division*, the box was to be buried under the building and the monument erected in his name. Now, was the monument *in* the building or just *near* it? Were the bones really buried under the building?

The monument, as described by Mrs. Sheffield, stood a few yards from the original grave that was now covered by the Ann & Hope Mill. In her own words, "It is of granite about twelve feet high, the base five or six feet square and the shaft a foot or more smaller, tapering slightly. It is within the enclosed grounds of the mill, surrounded by the vivid green of a beautiful lawn, being the only object on it."

The front has a cross on it marking the reverend as being buried there as well as noting his status as founder of Boston and the first white settler of Rhode Island. The other three sides boast the rest of his achievements during his life, when he settled in Rhode Island and when he died. The obelisk was pretty typical in the fashion of an honorary monument. As for his bones, a certain G.W. Pratt was entrusted to hold on to the wooden box until the mill was completed and the monument erected.

For many years, the remains of Reverend Blackstone rested with his monument in the industrial clamor of whirring engines and spindles. The monument sat a few yards away on the north side of the mill within the grounds of the compound. The "Spirit of the Gentle Sage" was most definitely out of his environment mixed among such a habitat in his eternal repose. The box remained untouched from 1889 to the 1940s, when the textile industry began a southward migration in search of cheaper labor. Ann & Hope's majestic walls soon held but memories and ghosts of the industrial revolution. As for the monument, the grass grew wild, and the stone fell into neglect.

This was short-lived, however. America was in the throes of World War II, and new life was soon given to the mill as a repair depot for the naval armory. Now there was a new dilemma for the monument. The hustle and bustle of trains loading and unloading military parts threatened its existence. The First Presbyterian Church of Cumberland entered into an agreement to move the monument onto a piece of its land for further preservation. The navy agreed, and in 1944, William Blackstone's monument was moved to its present location at the intersection of Broad and Cumberland Streets, a spot that overlooks the rear of the great mill. Were his remains moved with the monument? It was unclear whether they had been dug up and relocated. It was also unclear if they had ever been buried under the vast stone to begin with.

The Town of Cumberland now maintains the memorial park where the stone graces the small walkway around it. It looks slightly out of place sitting on a corner right next to a sidewalk overlooking what is now America's first discount store (you guessed it: Ann & Hope Discount Store). We can trace the elusive bones up to the 1960s, when James Furay—who was Ann & Hope's plant manager in the 1940s—was overseeing a digging project to

The roving memorial to William Blackstone is set in a permanent place, for now.

extend utilities to a newly constructed cottage that was to be used as an office. While digging, the backhoe ran into a box. It was sealed in heavy lead, and the corners had been soldered tight. Upon opening it, the crew found some bone fragments and very old nails. The box had been buried north of one of the north towers, which was razed during renovations to the mill.

The box sat in a storeroom until the 1960s, when Ann & Hope went through another expansion. Furay's old office and the storeroom were cleaned to make room for a new structural enclosure. Mr. Furay had intended to give the box to the Rhode Island Historical Society but somehow never got around to it. It obviously was not reburied under the monument when the obelisk was moved to its present location.

Did the small coffin containing Reverend Blackstone's remains get thrown out when the store was expanding? If so, then it is more than likely that Rhode Island's founder is now buried in the state landfill. Does that sound like a fitting way to bestow our gratitude for the great reverend who was the first white settler of our state, rode a bull and gave Rhode Island its famous apples? Some thanks!

PHINEAS G. WRIGHT

Many people leave lasting impressions on history with words they speak during their mortal reign on this earth. In the case of Mr. Phineas Gardner Wright, it is the words on his gravestone in Putnam's Grove Street Cemetery that caught the attention of many eyes and even pages of countless books throughout the last few centuries. The monument itself is a spectacle to behold—protruding from the side of the stone is a full-size granite bust of Mr. Wright, complete with a watch chain leading into his vest watch pocket, looking rather mystified as if reaffirming the now famous phrase below that reads, "Going. But know not where."

Phineas was born in Fitzwilliam, New Hampshire, on April 3, 1829. When he was a young lad, his family moved to Putnam, Connecticut, where he would spend the rest of his days as well as eternity. Phineas was a wealthy man. In fact, at one point he was the wealthiest in town. He had many land dealings according to town records. He amassed quite a fortune through hard work and typical Yankee frugality. This frugality was matched only by his eccentricity.

Legend has it that he did all of his banking in Boston so that none of the nosy locals would know exactly how much the man was worth. Perhaps he trusted none of the local banks and preferred the larger, stable banks of the great New England city. Either way, it was a good day's ride, a task that Phineas performed quite often.

Some recollections paint the man as a penny-pinching soul who wore old ragged clothes and rode a decrepit buckboard wagon pulled by a swaybacked nag. Research shows that Mr. Wright was a kinder, more generous being, one whose manner and dress fit into his station in life. This did not stop him from having a good sense of humor. When one peruses the old Putnam directories, next to his name is the space for an occupation, where it is noted, "Having no business, but minding my own."

The man professed to have broken the first ground in the construction of the historic Air Line Railway, which opened in 1873 as a direct train route between New York and Boston. The railway is now a hiking trail, but at one time, it was a promising enterprise complete with a "ghost train" (cars painted white with gold trim to attract wealthy customers) that ran from 1891 to 1895.

If Phineas lived a frugal lifestyle, it certainly would not be the case in the afterlife, for his burial marker is nothing short of spectacular. Fifteen years before he died, Wright set out to create his own burial marker and grave. Publications at the time swarmed in on the event, as it seemed quite unorthodox to prepare for the inevitable in such a way. The monument, weighing in at ten tons, was made by Worcester Monument Company for a cost of $1,000. Phineas traveled to Worcester several times to pose for the plaster cast that would be used for his bust. The bust was designed by A.R. Hewitt and cut by Mr. S. Ravidon. Two publications of the time tell the story in a brief and concise manner. An excerpt from the seventh volume of *The Successful American* notes, "Phineas G. Wright of Putnam, CT, one of the wealthiest residents of that town is now preparing his own tomb. He drew plans for it and is seeing that his contractor is carrying them out. He was born in 1829 in New Hampshire and boasts that his first dollar was made carrying the hod."

The January 1903 publication of *Granite*, volume 13, issue no. 1, notes that Phineas was a "hale and hearty" man. The excerpt further states that he was considered a good risk by many insurance companies. The next lines appear in both publications: "He informed the men at work on his monument that his grave was already dug and bricked and that those who assist in burying him will find liquid refreshments within." It seems that Mr. Wright filled the grave with libations as a reward for those who laid him in his final resting place to freely imbibe.

After the stone was completed, Phineas overheard some curious onlookers mention that the beard was too long. He then had the beard chiseled down not once but twice before he was satisfied with the creation. The grave sat empty for Phineas, who had no signs of illness or impending need to fulfill such a task at that time. Nonetheless, Phineas Gardner Wright later died on May 2, 1918, and was laid to rest in the eternal chamber he had designed fifteen years before. Scores of books have since been published that contain a page somewhere within adorned with the now world-famous phrase, "Going. But know not where." One can only wonder if Mr. Wright knows where now.

The famous stone of Phineas Gardner Wright in Putnam's Grove Street Cemetery.

One more fact that has never come to light should be noted in regard to claims of him being a miser and penny-pincher. He was a kind and generous man. A promissory note dated October 1, 1879, shows that George and Sarah Pray of Putnam owed Mr. Wright $700. As a result, the Pray family deeded their property to Phineas in the form of a fee simple transaction on January 30, 1880, until the debt was paid, with a 6 percent interest, collectable upon request. In the meantime, the family transferred the land between heirs without interference until May 10, 1902, when Mary Pray, daughter of George and Sarah, paid him the $700. Phineas then quitclaimed the land back to the Pray family, who had occupied it all along anyway. It seems that he decided not to charge any interest on the twenty-two-year-old debt, nor did he ever take the property away as payment for the promissory note. These do not sound like the actions of a miser but rather those of a man of a generous and kind nature.

You may wonder why we would defend this allegation so much. Well, we happen to own that particular piece of property. In fact, this whole book was written there.

THE DARN MAN'S ETERNAL CIRCUIT

In 1906, historian Ellen Larned put a request in several newspapers for information regarding a character called the "Darn Man" who once roamed the highways and byways of eastern Connecticut, southern Massachusetts and western Rhode Island. The number of replies she received from those who knew this wandering spirit was astounding, as were their recollections of this strange traveler. It is the remembrances of those people that may best tell of the mysterious, rambling pedestrian called the "Darn Man" or "Old Darn Coat."

As far as anyone knew, the Darn Man just appeared out of nowhere and continued his circuit with a ceaseless and precise regimen for fifty years, roaming from town to town in southeast New England.

George Griggs, who lived in Woodstock with his aunt, Mrs. Ebenezer Skinner, in about 1863, recounted his memories of the spring-heeled wanderer. The Darn Man was a regular visitor to the Skinner place, as was the case with many other homes along his route. One day in February of that year, young Griggs set out for the barn to complete the night's chores. A frightful snowstorm had blanketed the ground with a generous portion of the frosty precipitation. Mr. Griggs wrote this account in 1906:

> *I chanced to notice a bundle on the side of the snow path, and soon recognized it as the prostrate form of our monthly visitor. I aroused him and gently aided him to the house where my aunt fed and warmed him. He*

remained with us for three days. My aunt had a good room and bed always reserved for his accommodations.

This was a common thread with the Darn Man, as you will see in this next account, written by Ellen Larned in her query to the masses for information on this strange fellow:

Many years ago, a weird figure was often seen hurrying along the roads and byways of Windham County, spectral and gaunt with bent form and long white hair, heedless of passerby or curious query, pausing at some accustomed farmhouse for needle and thread to darn his much worn suit and for food and a night's lodging.

Miss Larned received numerous replies from those whose families saw and entertained the curious eccentric.

W.B. Fox of Norwich added to Miss Larned's declaration by stating that while living in Hampton, Connecticut, the Darn Man used to visit his home quite often. He would never beg for anything but needles and thread to darn his suit, which by that time was already a mass of many varied colors and threads from previous repairs. When he wanted to eat, he would walk into the kitchen and seat himself at the table of some familiar house, and to Mr. Fox's knowledge, he was never refused anything he wanted. It was told that someone once asked him, "Why don't you go home? Where is your home anyway?" He replied, "Anywhere the night overtakes me, if they will please let me stay." The man welcomed him into his home and never questioned his occasional guest again.

Thomas Bennett of Canterbury recalled the old Darn Man making his way into town twice a year, calling for needle and thread with which he would darn the rents in his coat and other places that were not worn as well. Mr. Bennett's father was a shoemaker. Bennett reminisced how the old Darn Man would enter his father's shop, take the worn heels off his shoes and replace them himself. The Darn Man was an avid tea drinker, as attested to by all of the parties who kept company with him.

A Windham County woman wrote a recollection of her encounters with the Darn Man for a literary society in 1889:

This strange name belonged to a tall white figure, whose rapid, gliding step and ghostly appearance made one question whether he was really of this world and not some visitor from the realms of shadow. I remember him as an old man, his form slightly bowed, his long white hair falling down his neck, his earnest look forward, never seeming to notice anyone as he passed along…

He stopped at certain places and with the elegance of a Chesterfield, asked for some slight refreshment, or for a cup of tea. None had higher appreciation of the merits of the fragrant beverage. With a canister of the best tea given him, he would make a cup that a celestial would enjoy.

He was very exclusive in his choice of stops, having only those who were honored to receive his company be part of his regular sojourns.

Mr. A.D. Ayer recounted much about the Darn Man, including his fondness for tea. He very often prepared the beverage himself, making it quite strong, and would drink several cups, sampling each one until it suited his taste. Mr. Ayer also recollected the legend attributing to his unusual lifestyle. This story has been passed down and altered by raconteurs to fit their narrations, but the main essence seems to be that he was to be married but his bride died suddenly, leaving him waiting literally at the altar in his wedding suit. It was this suit that he wore to her funeral and this suit that he wore and darned incessantly the rest of his wandering days. It is generally accepted that he took to his peripatetic circuit after the death of his betrothed because of a mental breakdown suffered from that fateful day. Some claim that he walked the byways of the region in a never-ending search for his lost bride after that.

Mr. Ayer described what he knew of the Darn Man in the second volume of *A Modern History of Windham County, Connecticut* by Allen B. Lincoln. From April 1859 to about 1860, the Darn Man appeared regularly at Ayer's home in Hampton, also known as Goshen and Clark's Corners. His mother received bits and pieces of the traveler's life during these visits. Mr. Ayer reported:

He had on that same coat he was wearing when he went to a certain place—he would not say whether it was a church or a house—to be married. The bride never came; he never knew what became of her. He then said he would never wear any other coat until he found her. So as time went on, when a hole or tear came, he darned it with many colored threads, strings and yarns; hence his name, old "Darn Coat." He usually wore a tall or stovepipe hat, in which he carried his glasses, kerchief, and a nice snuffbox with gold inlaid in the cover, which a woman had given him years before I knew him, and in the snuffbox was the bean which all snuff users had in their boxes. He was a man who was well posted in current events and past history. He was a great reader. My father had a regular reading list, the Hartford Weekly Times, New York Ledger (Bonner's), Harper's Illustrated Weekly, occasionally, the Boston True Flag, Saturday Evening Post (Philadelphia), and mother had Ladies' Magazine. The "darn man" asked, soon after he began to come to our house, if he could not work a little and stay two or three days, so that he could read more. He seemed to be much interested in mother's magazine. He would call her attention to a woman in a new style of dress, and then would sit down and gaze at it for a long time. Mother would ask him if it carried him back to the young woman he expected to marry when he saw those pictures, and he would say, "If I told you, you would know my thoughts, my memories of the past." Never would he give a straight answer.

It is known that the Darn Man was also musically inclined. Mr. Ayer, along with a few others who knew the itinerant, was occasionally given concerts on the violin by the man. Although the Ayer family never found out his real name or place of birth, they suspected that he might have been of English origin as he spoke of the country and people as if he had firsthand knowledge. His visits were regular, arriving once a month from April to January. Where he was in the interim months was a mystery to the family. He was also known to be neat and well groomed. He always cleaned himself and his garb whenever possible. Mr. Ayer went on to state:

At times he carried an umbrella—he must have picked it up—quite a bit of money, for he had some with him. He would talk about the way English people did in order to get on the throne and was especially down on queens, relating their treachery, for example, Mary and her sister, telling how you can trust some women, their word is good, but most of them are only for themselves. He would turn to me and say, "Boy, as you grow up, beware of the girls. Don't spend your money on them. Don't pay out for a nice wedding suit, especially a coat, for you may be left as I was, to wander about with my wedding coat I avowed to wear until I learned what became of the one whom I had adored, who I am not willing to say went back on me; I am charitable enough to think she was spirited away or lost her mind and perhaps was killed."

He told the family that his name was Thompson and that he had two brothers who were farmers. He mentioned that he hailed from New Bedford.

After the family left Hampton and moved to Scotland, Connecticut, they saw the Darn Man a few more times, and when asked why he did not change

The old dirt road at the Connecticut/Rhode Island line where the Darn Man was found frozen but alive in November 1863. The gravel lane has not changed much over the centuries.

his route to pay them visits at their new home, he replied, "No, I have my mind made up to keep on going over the same route, in the same towns, and I expect to die some time in some of the places I have been for years."

When asked if he would, in confidence, reveal the names of some relatives who might be contacted in the event of his passing or who might receive any money he had as an inheritance, he merely stated, "If you knew what I know about myself, you would know what I know."

Allen Jewett, also of Hampton, recalled how the Darn Man often stayed at his father's home. He described him as tall and slender, with small features, thin hands and blue eyes. He wore a swallowtail coat, tightfitting pants and a vest, along with his stovepipe hat. He drank lots of tea but ate little. He told Mr. Jewett's mother that his name was George Johnson and that he had two sisters living in Rhode Island.

The Darn Man was quite a tea aficionado. He would always ask for a cup at his stops; in fact, he carried a cloth in which to wrap tea leaves. He often would ask the lady of the house if he could prepare the beverage to his liking. If he stayed the night, he would have breakfast and, without hesitation, stand and bid a grateful thank-you before setting out once again on his journey.

As for the stories explaining his wanderings, they range from his bride dying at sea upon returning with her wedding dress to leaving him standing at the altar. Another notes that he was to be married in New London, but his betrothed died of a sudden sickness. According to the man, she never showed up for the wedding and was never heard from again, which is why he wandered, ceaselessly marching the same circuit, searching for his bride.

As time wore on, the spring in the Darn Man's stride wore down. His gait became less enthusiastic; his tall, slender figure became hunched over with age; and his youthful look became scarred with sunken, saddened eyes. He died in late November 1863 on a road between Sterling, Connecticut, and Foster, Rhode Island. Elisha Anderson found him frozen but alive on the side of the road and assisted in carrying the old man to his farmhouse. Unfortunately, the Darn Man did not make it to the home before passing. It is reported that Mr. Anderson buried the man in the family lot. It was later revealed that the man's name was Addison Thompson, but some state that it was Moses Thompson; others insist that he was Frank Howland, descendant of the *Mayflower* Howlands.

Whoever the Darn Man really was may be shrouded in mystery for all time. My attempts to find his identity have consistently reached a dead end. I have researched each name and found that there is no substantial evidence that any of those names represented the true identity of the extraordinary figure known as the "Darn Man" or "Old Darn Coat."

THE INDIAN GHOST OF
HANNAH FRANK

Burrillville is the second-largest town in Rhode Island and home to many legends and haunts. Its picturesque colonial landscape still defies the onslaught of time and progress. The town is situated in the northwest portion of the Ocean State, which is why the town's historical society's motto is "We Have History in Our Corner." No area in Burrillville is more picturesque (or haunted) than the Tarkiln section of town. This bucolic country hamlet is laced with historic homes along the few back roads, and the woods boast of the ruins of several old factories and mills, ripe with accounts of restless spirits from the past.

These alone are a sight to behold, but it does not end there. Tarkiln is also home to Burrillville's most famous specter: the Indian ghost of Hannah Frank. Frank is said to eternally haunt the woods of Tarkiln in search of justice for her murder and her prized necklace, given to her by her betrothed before they were brutally slain on the night of September 18, 1831.

Legends are often reared and weaned from the bottle of truth. The stories become larger than life itself, taking on wholly different demeanors that result in the metamorphosis of an account into a tale barely resembling its factual counterpart. The story of Hannah Frank and John Burke has been painted in ink as a romantic tale of love, courtship and romance ending in tragedy, much like a modern Romeo and Juliet. In my own research through old papers and interviews with historians, I have heard the same tale over and over. This is the legend I write first, the one you will be familiar with. However, I am compelled to pen another version,

The hand-hewn headstones and footstones of Hannah Frank and John Burke in the woods of Tarkiln mark the spot where Hannah was found. This is also the area that is haunted by her ghost.

the one that comes from the mouth of a condemned man with his last mortal breaths, knowing well that he would meet his maker for the crimes for which he swore he was innocent. The account you are about to read is what has been the popular ghost story for at least a century. This is what has been related to me as the hard truth for more than twenty years—a truth I now must take as legend rather than fact. Oh yes, there is a ghost, but for what justice does she cry?

Hannah Frank was a nineteen-year-old Nipmuc Indian who worked as a housekeeper for Amasa E. Walmsley and his younger brother, Thomas J., who were Nipmuc as well. A peddler from Vermont named John Burke came down on occasion to the thriving community to sell his wares and met Hannah on one of his visits to the house. He fell head over heels for her and gave her a gift. A courtship followed.

To say that the Walmsley brothers were not pleased with this courtship would be an understatement. When Burke showed up on their property, he was immediately forced to leave. This did not stop Hannah and her suitor from enjoying time together, as they met in the center of town to court and carry on with their love affair. Every trip down from Vermont was followed by another endowment to the young and beautiful Hannah. Her most prized gift of all was a beautiful shell necklace that she never removed from her neck.

Then came September 18, 1831, the day when John Burke proposed to Hannah and offered to take her back to his home in Vermont as his bride. Her acceptance was met with concealed rage from the Walmsley brothers, who were opposed to her relationship with Burke. Whether it was prejudice or the fact that the Walmsleys wanted Hannah for themselves has never been divulged. At any rate, the brothers outwardly wished them well and even celebrated with them at the Walmsley house. After much drink and merriment, Hannah packed up her belongings, and the two set out that afternoon down Log Road for a new life together.

The trip was short-lived. Amasa and Thomas intercepted them at the corner of Log Road and Horse Head Trail and brutally attacked the couple. John Burke ran east down Horse Head Trail in an attempt to divert the brothers from Hannah but was caught a few hundred yards away and beheaded on the spot with an axe. The two then caught up with Hannah, who had managed to flee in the opposite direction on Horse Head Trail. They began to beat her with their fists and a stick. One account goes as far as stating that Thomas Walmsley killed Hannah with a single blast from his shotgun. During the attack, her beloved necklace was somehow torn from her neck. As the very juice of life bled from her body, she managed to crawl up against a great pine tree where, before the day could pass, she died.

The bodies of John Burke and Hannah Frank were found several days later by search parties. Several witnesses had seen Amasa wearing a shirt with bloodstains on it, and each time he was questioned as to their origin, he gave conflicting accounts. The murders were finally brought to light when a suspicious J.D. Nichols, owner of one of the largest mills in the village, coerced the truth out of his housekeeper, who was the sister of the Walmsley brothers. Amasa and Thomas were arrested and tried on separate occasions. Amasa confessed to the crime and was sentenced according to a *Providence Journal* article dated April 3, 1832, by Chief Justice Eddy to "Be Hanged by the Neck Till You Are Dead! And may God have mercy on your soul." Amasa E. Walmsley swung from the end of a rope for the murders on June 1, 1832. It was the first hanging carried out by the State of Rhode Island at Field Point. His brother, Thomas, was arraigned on September 1, 1832. After a brief trial, he was also found guilty of the murder of John Burke and the aiding of Amasa in the murder of Hannah Frank.

The following is a portion of the actual sentencing of Thomas J. Walmsley:

The sentence of the court is, that you the said Thomas J. Walmsley be taken hence to the prison from whence you came. That you be taken thence on Friday the eighth day of February next, to the place of execution to be appointed by the sheriff of the county of Providence, in said county; and that you there, between the hour of nine and twelve of the clock in the forenoon of the same day, be hanged by the neck till you are dead. And may God have mercy on your soul!!!

Another part of the legend often related is that Thomas died in a fall from an oxcart before he could be brought to justice—a portion of the story made up over time to create a situation ripe for a haunting, no doubt.

Neighbors and friends buried the couple next to the spot where Hannah died. They fashioned four fieldstones into headstones and footstones by rounding off the tops and smoothing one side. The stones still stand among the brush five hundred feet west of Log Road across from the old WLKW radio towers on private property.

Hannah's ghost is frequently seen roaming the woods where she was killed, looking for her adored necklace and lost love. Residents of Log Road have witnessed her apparition during various hours of the day and night. The Woonsocket Sportsman's Club is presently located down Horse Head Trail. Members of the club say that her spirit has been spotted at dusk in the woods. She has also been spied a few yards into the trail from Log Road, wandering to and fro, as if she were endlessly searching for something. Others have heard a faint voice carried by the wind relaying what sounds like, "Where is my necklace?" Sometimes the recipients of her whispers hear her say, "my justice."

A riveting story it is. I became completely drawn into this tale when many of the pieces did not seem to fit. It took a few years, but I have managed to find some interesting documentation and historical data that may make you think twice about what you just read.

Yes, the two were found dead about eighty rods from each other (a rod equals sixteen and a half feet) and were buried where Hannah was found. And yes, she does haunt the woods, but lets straighten out a few facts.

Hannah Frank was actually a mulatto woman who was a distant relation to the Walmsleys. Thomas Walmsley Sr. was a "mustee" or half-breed of the Narragansett tribe. He married an Indian named Nancie Pike. Their household was listed in the 1790 state census for Smithfield as having seven "free persons of color." Amasa was born in Burrillville on August 24, 1806. Mr. Walmsley died when Amasa was about ten years old. From there, Amasa wandered around from farm to farm as a laborer. His two other brothers and three sisters lived in Rhode Island and Connecticut. His mother later married a Brayton and moved to Jewett City, Connecticut. Amasa and his brother Thomas stayed close by each other in Burrillville.

When Amasa was condemned to the gallows, he wrote a pamphlet called "Life and Confession of Amasa E. Walmsley." Stephen Wilmarth was present to pen the story and made sure that Amasa got everything he said printed as it was related.

The first several pages are a plea to all about the effects of intemperance and intoxication. He tells of how his family was drawn to the bottle and how he found alcohol to be a favorable beverage even as an infant. Having stated his cause, he went on to tell that he was accused of having murdered an "Irishman named John Burke and a mulatto woman named Hannah Frank."

According to Walmsley, the couple lived in the woods of Burrillville doing odd jobs for money and making occasional nightly raids on neighboring farms for provisions. He described them as "leading a most disorderly and beastly life of debauchery and intemperance."

Hannah, being a distant relation to the Walmsleys, sometimes stayed at his uncle Elisha Newfield's home in the colder months. Burke was mostly unknown to him, having only met him a few times. Although he did not care for his company or acquaintance, he did state that on no occasion did he ever turn an angry word or gesture toward him. "If we were not on intimate terms, I certainly wished him no ill, and as I had no reason to be a foe to him, he probably was not a foe to me."

On the night of September 18, 1831, Amasa and Thomas spent several hours imbibing spirits at the store of Rufus Smith in Burrillville. At about 9:30 p.m., they set out for home. Having arrived at Thomas's house between 10:00 and 11:00 p.m., they found Hannah, John and what he termed a "dissolute and most abandoned girl" by the name of Fidelia Ketch visiting with his family. They, too, had been drinking all night and were in merry spirits. The three seemed glad to see Amasa and his brother and invited them to share in their liquor. The party lasted until late in the evening; everyone sang and danced together in general good jest. At no time did Amasa ever imagine a quarrel between them.

When Hannah and John left, Fidelia proposed that the three of them chase down Hannah and John and beat them, for she accused Hannah of stealing some of her clothes. Both Thomas and Amasa refused, stating that the couple had done them no wrong, but under the insistence of Ketch, they agreed to accompany her.

They followed behind the vengeful woman, who had dressed in their clothing to disguise herself. When they caught up to the couple, Fidelia hit Hannah with a rock, knocking her to the ground, and she then struck her several more times. Amasa took a stick and began hitting John Burke, who fell from either the blows or his drunken state. Amasa struck John several more times with a pine stick that he described as incapable of causing injury, let alone death. During the fight, John produced the spout of a coffeepot, declaring that it was a pistol and that he was going to shoot Amasa. Amasa hit him one more time and then backed off. According to Amasa, John and Hannah were very much alive and groaning when they left them.

After several days, they had not heard anything from the couple, but this was not unusual, as the two lived in the desolation of the forest away from civilization. It was Thomas who told Amasa that they had been found dead in the woods in two different locations eighty rods from each other. By the time the brothers arrived, the bodies had been placed in coffins for interment. Neither gave any thought that they might be accused of the deed. A few days later, Amasa was arrested and charged but later released on unsubstantial and insignificant evidence.

It was Ketch who would make some sort of confession, resulting in a second arrest. This time, Amasa was put on trial in March 1832 and found guilty. His brother would later suffer the same fate.

The court transcript from Monday, March 3, 1832, notes that Amasa E. Walmsley and Thomas J. Walmsley, both laborers of Burrillville, willfully beat Hannah Frank upon the head and above and near the right eye with a "stick of no value," causing a fatal wound the length of two inches long by one quarter inch wide and deep. Records also indicate that she was thrown, kicked, punched and received several mortal wounds about the head, breast, back, belly, sides, arms and legs. This is in gross contrast to what Amasa claimed happened the night of September 18 and a far cry from the legend as we know it.

Thomas was put on trial for killing John Burke, referred to as a "foreigner," and aiding his brother in the murder of Hannah Frank. He was found guilty on September 26, 1832, and executed on February 8, 1833. Whatever happened to Fidelia Ketch remains a mystery. There are no birth or death records of Fidelia for that period, and no census records verify her existence. The 1830 census for Burrillville also mentions Thomas Walmsley and six others in his household as "Free Colored Persons." This suggests that Amasa may have lived with Thomas at the time, since two of them were between the ages of twenty-four and thirty-six.

A view down Horse Head Trail, where Hannah Frank and John Burke were accosted on September 18, 1831, by Amasa and Thomas Walmsley and Fidelia Ketch.

What also seems suspicious is that Ketch wanted to wear the brothers' clothes to attack a drunken couple in the dark of night. Why did she require such a disguise? Did she go back to finish what she started? Were the Walmsleys actually innocent of murder? How did Hannah Frank and John Burke come to be found so far from each other? Was it the work of a wild animal? Any of these could be the reason why Hannah roams the woods to this day.

Beth Williams, daughter of longtime Tarkiln resident Sheila Williams, witnessed the frightening apparition of Hannah Frank in the woods on several occasions with others when they lived near the trail and walked it frequently. The first time she saw it, she was with her cousin. They both became very frightened by the apparition and ran. It followed them, vanishing only when they screamed out of fear. After that, she got used to the idea of what she called the "Indian Princess" randomly appearing in the woods near her home.

My wife, Arlene, and I have visited the sight on numerous occasions, as we once lived in one of the historic homes of Tarkiln. One strange incident I encountered was when we were there one evening near dusk, and I was walking a few yards into the woods to take a picture. As I focused the shot, I heard a whisper behind me and turned quickly only to see what one might call a shadow person move out of the corner of my eye and quickly disappear. The woods are sparse enough to see well into the distance, so if it had been an animal, I would have seen it run off. It was gone before I could get a picture of it. Photos of the wooded area showed no ghost. The whisper caught me by surprise. Maybe it was just my imagination, or perhaps it was Hannah saying, "my necklace" or "my justice." The voice was very distinct and close to my ear. I must admit that it momentarily startled me enough to miss the exact phrase.

If it was the spirit of Hannah Frank I encountered, then I am one of the many people who have witnessed the ghost forever doomed to roam the woods of Tarkiln. Whether she is in search of justice or her beloved necklace and suitor, the "Indian Princess" is now a permanent and welcome fixture in the eyes of local residents, who sometimes watch and listen for the girl in search of the necklace, justice or at least an attempt to hold on to the life that she lost at an early age.

So, which account do you prefer to hold dear to your heart? The long-told legend or the written accounts found in historical documents? Perhaps the truth lies somewhere in between. It could be that someone returned to the scene to finish off the couple after the Walmsley brothers had gone to sleep off their intemperance. Perhaps Hannah seeks justice for her real murderer. The story has become a bit more fascinating, don't you think?

What Is a Yankee Doodle?

One of the most popular American songs in the history of our nation actually began as an insult to our forefathers. British troops used the song "Yankee Doodle" to mock and insult the Americans. A "Yankee" was a term for backwoods New Englanders, and the word "doodle" was German for "fool" or "simpleton." It first appeared in the seventeenth century as *dudel* or *dodel*. Macaroni was the term of the day for a dandy or fop. The famous first verse implies that the Yankees were so crude that they thought that by sticking a feather in their cap, they would be thought of as fashionable and witty. So, you have a song about backwoods simpletons trying to look sophisticated as a praise of our people, right? Well, not exactly, but that is how it began.

The origin of the song can be traced back to 1755 during the French and Indian War. A British army surgeon, Dr. Richard Shuckburgh, wrote the lyrics after seeing the colonial troops serving under Colonel Thomas Finch Jr., son of Connecticut governor Thomas Finch. Colonel Finch and his ragtag group of militia were about to set out from his homestead in Norwalk, Connecticut, to rally with troops at Fort Crailo in Rensselaer, New York. The colonel's sister, Elizabeth, came out of the house and stopped them. "You have no matching uniforms or anything to let everyone know you are of the same company." She then went into the chicken yard, plucked some chicken feathers and had the soldiers position them in their hats. "There." She said. "You must have uniforms of some kind."

When the company arrived at Fort Crailo, Dr. Shuckburgh took one look at the plumes in their hats and was reported to have said, "Now stab my vitals, they're macaronis!" He then immediately penned the now famous tune.

Another tale of the name's origin is in regard to the Crown. When Oliver Cromwell came to visit Oxford, he rode a small horse while wearing a hat with a large, fancy plume protruding from its band. The royalists called the plumed figure "macaroni," and the townsfolk joked that he looked like a dandy.

The English were quick to adopt new lyrics to the song from the start, borrowing the melody from the nursery rhyme "Lucy Locket." Their versions started out as a joke aimed at the disorganized colonial Yankees and their makeshift uniforms, but after the Seven Years' War and right up until the end of the Revolution, the song took on a malevolent tone. The verses geared toward the ridicule of the American leaders made the Yankees grit their teeth and clench their fists. There is speculation that before the Boston Massacre, British soldiers taunted the colonists by singing a few verses of their own version of the song. During the march to Boston from Concord on April 15, 1775, the British sang it to a marching rhythm. It was also sung at the Battle of Breed's Hill. As the rebel forces began to take control over the British, the Yankees claimed the song as their own and quickly made up verses praising their victories and mocking the British and the king.

When Cornwallis surrendered, the Americans sang "Yankee Doodle" with sarcastic pride. The song instantly became the unofficial national anthem. The most widely adapted version of the song consists of about sixteen verses. The popularity of the melody carried over to the Civil War, where both sides made up verses to taunt their enemies.

Although the origin of the phrase has taken on several forms, it can be concluded by its widespread use during the war for independence and beyond that the name became a common moniker of the day regarding certain persons, as well as a symbol of American pride in more contemporary years. Yankee Doodle, keep it up.

New England's First
Witch Execution

Salem, Massachusetts, is the witch capital of America. The now infamous witchcraft trials took place in 1692, and within the course of several months, countless people were arrested, jailed and tried for allegedly making pacts with the devil. In the end, nineteen people were hanged, three died in jail and one man, Giles Corey, was pressed to death. Although this is remembered as a monumental moment in New England history, little notice is given to the first known execution of a witch in the New World. New England's first executed witch was not born in Salem but rather in a small place called Windsor, Connecticut. Little is actually known about Alse Young (sometimes called Achsuh or Alice), and less would have been if she were not accused of being in league with Satan.

In 1642, the Connecticut colony made witchcraft a crime punishable by death. The offense was backed by several verses in the King James version of the Bible, such as Exodus 22:18, where it is written, "Thou shalt not suffer a witch to live." Also Leviticus 20:27 notes, "A man also or woman that hath a familiar spirit, or that is a wizard, shall surely be put to death." Witchcraft was listed as a capital crime in 1715 but was taken off the list when the laws were rewritten in 1750.

Alse Young, born circa 1600, was accused of being a witch and was hanged in 1647 at the Meetinghouse Square in Hartford, Connecticut, now the site of the Old Statehouse. Her crime was reported to be nothing more than preparing herbal remedies for her fellow colonists. Alse is thought to have been the wife of John Young, a settler who owned a small tract of land in Windsor. He bought the land in 1641 and sold it in 1649, two years after Alse's death. After that, he dissappeared from town records. Their one daughter, Alice Young Beamon, would also be accused of witchcraft thirty years later while residing in Springfield, Massachusetts.

There are two outstanding written records of Alse Young's execution for witchcraft. One is from the second town clerk of Windsor, Matthew Grant, who noted in a diary on May 26, 1647, "Alse Young was hanged." The other comes from none other than Massachusetts Bay Colony governor John Winthrop, who wrote in his journal, "One [illegible] of Windsor arraigned and executed at Hartford for a witch."

This event took place forty-five years before the Salem hysteria of 1692. From 1647 to 1697, there were roughly forty-five known cases from Connecticut. The last executions of these known cases took place in 1662 with the executions of Rebecca and Nathaniel Greensmith, Mary Sanford and Mary Barnes.

If you are wondering when the first actual case of witchcraft took place, it was recorded in 1638 in Boston, Massachusetts. Jane Hawkins, a midwife, was accused of practicing witchcraft when she assisted in the birth of Mary Dyer's child. Midwives were used quite frequently in colonial times and are still found today. A midwife not only helped in the delivery of a child but also played the role of healer, nurse and therapist. When necessary, they would also be the ones to perform an abortion. The mortality rate of both the mother and the child was dangerously high, and a good midwife was always in demand.

Such knowledge and power was looked on with suspicion in the eyes of the religious, especially in Puritan New England, where the practice was carried over from England (along with the suspicion). In this case, Mary Dyer and Jane Hawkins were Antinomians, followers of Anne Hutchinson, who was banished from the Massachusetts Bay Colony for her religious diversions.

On October 17, Hawkins helped deliver the child, a stillborn and premature fetus seen only by Hutchinson, Dyer, Hawkins and another woman, who termed the child a "monster," as written in John Winthrop's journal. Winthrop questioned the midwife, who stated that the child was born mishapen and buried shortly after. He went on to write:

> *The governor, with advice of some other of the magistrates and of the elders of Boston, caused the said monster to be taken up, and though it were much corrupted, yet most of those things were to be seen, as the horns and claws, the scales, etc. When it died in the mother's body, (which was about*

two hours before the birth,) the bed whereon the mother lay did shake, and withal there was such a noisome savor, as most of the women were taken with extreme vomiting and purging, so as they were forced to depart; and others of them their children were taken with convulsions, (which they never had before nor after), and so were sent for home, so as by these occasions it came to be concealed.

Another thing observable was, the discovery of it, which was just when Mrs. Hutchinson was cast out of the church. For Mrs. Dyer going forth with her, a stranger asked, what young woman it was. The others answered, it was the woman which had the monster; which gave the first occasion to some that heard it to speak of it. The midwife, presently after this discovery, went out of the jurisdiction; and indeed it was time for her to be gone, for it was known, that she used to give young women oil of mandrakes and other stuff to cause conception; and she grew into great suspicion to be a witch, for it was credibly reported, that, when she gave any medicines, (for she practised physic), she would ask the party, if she did believe, she could help her, etc.

This is the first known written accusation for witchcraft in the colonies. Winthrop's journal is a good source for what life was like at the dawn of the European colonization of present-day America.

The Curse of Micah Rood's Apples

This little tale of New England's myths and mysteries is one of my favorite stories of the region. It is also true. Sit back and raise the flame on your lantern so you can see the shadows dancing on the walls as you read about the cursed apples of Franklin, Connecticut.

Many do not believe in curses. They seem to believe that such vexes were born in bedtime tales designed to keep children fearfully in their beds long after the lights were drawn. In Franklin, many of the old-timers not only believe in curses, but some of them have actually ingested the remnants from one peculiar act of vengeance wrought upon a man more than three centuries ago. There is a place where an apple tree once bore fruit that contained what appeared to be a single drop of blood in the center of each one. Do not look for the tree now, as it is long gone, but the legend and accounts that follow will live as eternal reminders of the price of greed and murder.

Micah Rood was a farmer in what was once called Nine Mile Square or Norwich-West-Farms but is presently called Franklin. His farm rambled along the Peck Hollow section of the settlement. Youngest son of Thomas Rood, Micah came to settle here in either 1693 or 1699 (records differ on the exact date) and immediately set up his homestead. He was not greatly successful at his toils, but the land gave him enough to survive and barter the extra for other needed items. By some accounts, Rood was reported to be a friendly, outgoing man who gave his time to help anyone in need. That may have been one of the reasons for his lack of prosperity in both his farming and his funds. Others say that he was a mean and nasty brute who would just as soon shoot any person in need than offer a scrap to eat. One thing was certain: Rood's apples were the finest and best tended in the region.

One December evening, a peddler named Horgan passed along the edge of Rood's farm. The peddler was no stranger to the region. Many housewives and working gentry eagerly awaited his semiannual visits to see what wares he had in his bag for sale to the good people of the town. Back in the seventeenth, eighteenth and even nineteenth centuries, peddlers were common shopping middlemen. These roving stores wandered the countryside, selling everything from pots and pans to trinkets and jewelry. Horgan seemed to have a fine array of items that would make almost any man want to rifle through his sack. The itinerant peddler, by all known accounts, had sold much of his wares that day and possessed a hefty pouch of money collected from his sales. The next accounts are surely matters of conjecture as to what transpired next. Some say that the peddler, on a roll, decided to try his luck at Rood's home, while others claim that he was coerced into the home by Rood for unsavory reasons. Either way, the peddler was found the next day under one of Rood's apple trees with his head split open, his sack empty and his money pouch gone.

All fingers pointed toward Rood, but he vehemently denied any wrongdoing. In fact, he brought to the attention of the authorities two men who had attempted to waylay the traveling salesman at the Blue Horse Tavern the day before. Rood even let the authorities search his home, and they found no sign of any violence or the peddler's money. Horgan was buried in the potter's field, and although the villagers strongly believed that Rood had something to do with his demise, they soon let it go, for the time being.

Spring wore on, and Rood's farm began to prosper. It appeared that Rood had somehow caught a windfall in newfound wealth. No one could prove that Rood had killed the peddler, but nature was about to throw a strange light on the suspicions about Rood.

When the flowers bloomed, the apple trees blossomed with their usual sweet-smelling white flowers, with the exception of one tree. The tree where the peddler was found bore red petals. Although odd, no one gave it much of a second thought until August brought the fruits of labor forth. The townsfolk were quite astonished when they found that the apples that came from that particular tree in Rood's orchard had a curious nature to them. When broken open, there was a red globule in the center that resembled a drop of blood. Every apple on that tree seemed to contain within the bloodstain of the man who was murdered so hideously. All the other trees bore normal fruit. The people began to call them "mikes," for although they concealed the strange crimson blot within, they were unusually delicious.

As for Rood, he began a slow and mysterious deterioration in both physical and mental health. The once vivacious soul had become a frail recluse, fearful and melancholy. He refused to eat and began wasting away. Neighbors reported hearing his screams in the night, and when they crept up to his window, they could see him pacing to and fro in the darkest hours in front of a solitary candle. Within a short time, his farm died, and his will to live went with it. Yet there was the apple tree. Year after year, it bore the silent damnation in the form of the apples with bloody hearts. Many believed that the peddler's spirit had come to roost on the branches of the tree, thus tainting the fruit it bore. One season, a daring youth stole into Rood's orchard and began to loot the infamous tree of its harvest. Rood offered him all of the tree's fruit, screeching to the boy, "Take the whole lot, boy, I don't want the accursed things." Rood's condition worsened, and his fences fell into ruin. His barn decayed and swayed with the valley breezes that swept through the countryside. It is said that he was terrified to work in the fields, for the wraith of the peddler was always waiting there to torture him for his deed.

In 1717, Rood was given the task of maintaining the meetinghouse, and in return, the townsfolk compensated him with a peck of corn from each family in the congregation. Having long given up on living, his torturous existence continued, yet no confession came from his lips as to what happened to the peddler Horgan so many years ago. The bloody apples still poured from the tree that sat on the once fertile land now overgrown with brush and bramble.

In 1727, it came to pass that Rood needed constant attention, as he had become too feeble to care for himself. A historic record entered into the church society states as follows, "July 5, 1727. The inhabitants do now, by their vote, agree to allow each man that watches with Micah Rood, two shillings per night. Also to those who have attended to sd Rood by day, three shillings per day." Micah Rood finally passed away in December 1728. It is written that he died in a chair overlooking the cursed tree that bore the bloody fruit of vengeance. On December 17, 1728, the society paid four shillings to Jacob Hyde for digging Rood's grave.

The tree, however, lasted as a living monument to the unsolved crime for two more centuries, still bearing forth its peculiar harvest until the hurricane of 1938 finally blew down the centuries-old relic. Several attempts were made to cultivate the "mikes" by cutting and splicing the branches and

A typical New England apple tree in an orchard similar to what Micah Rood's now extinct "mike" tree may have looked like.

roots with other strains, but there is no record as to whether anyone ever successfully reproduced the apples that silently and eternally condemned Micah Rood for his alleged evil deed. Some say that there are trees that were grafted successfully and bear traces of the bloody apple. Take a ride into Franklin and visit some of the orchards around harvest time. Maybe, just maybe, you will find an apple with a blood-red heart. If so, then it is clear that the curse of Micah Rood is still alive in those delicious apples that gave so many taste buds pleasure and one man eternal pain.

The Legend of the
Kennebunk Inn

In the autumn of 2002, my wife, Arlene, and I stayed at one of the most charming places we have ever spent the night: the Kennebunk Inn on 45 Main Street in Kennebunk, Maine. The original section is more than two hundred years old, and yes, it is haunted. We were given the Fireplace Room of that section. This is the only private room with a fireplace and was the original bedroom of the house built by Phineas Cole for a doctor in 1799. At the time of our visit, it was owned by John and Kristen Martin, but it is now in the care of Brian and Shanna Horner O'Hea. Its spectral past, however, traces back to the 1950s, when a night clerk named Silas Perkins died in the very room we were given for our stay. It is said that he was brought to the room after suffering a heart attack in the street. It was probably done so the fire in the hearth could give him some comfort in his last moments on this earth. Silas spent his last minutes in that room, as well as, apparently, his eternal afterlife. It seems that he has never left the inn.

Built as a private residence in 1799, it was sold to Benjamin Smith in 1804. In 1876, Dr. Orrin Ross purchased the building. His son, Dr. Frank Ross, then owned it from 1880 until his death in 1926. It was sold in 1928 to Mr. George Baitler, who turned the private residence into a hotel named The Tavern. It was Mr. Baitler who added the two-and-a-half-story wing to the building, expanding its accommodations to fifty guest rooms. Sources say that the addition was a barn on the property that was moved and attached to the existing home. In the late 1930s, Walter Day purchased the building and renamed it the Kennebunk Inn. Not long after that, Silas Perkins became

The Kennebunk Inn on Main Street in Kennebunk, Maine.

the night clerk. He worked there for many years, with his desk in the room just above an old staircase in the cellar leading to nowhere, next to where the bar is now located.

In 1980, Arthur and Angela LeBlanc purchased the inn and renovated it to twenty-two rooms. It seems that this renovation awoke the spirit of Mr. Perkins, which began protesting the change. A bartender, Pattie Farnsworth, once had a visit from the spirit while transporting provisions from the basement, where she suddenly felt aware of a strange presence. Intuitively, the name "Cyrus" materialized in her mind, and the ghost was thus dubbed with that moniker. Soon after, ghostly antics became a common occurrence, and Cyrus was given all the blame.

A waitress carrying a tray of glasses once stared in shock as the wine glass in the center of the tray rose above the rest with no visible hand to hoist it. The glass then dropped to the floor in front of the waitress and some surprised diners who were present to witness the phenomenon. A bartender by the name of Dudley, minding his own business and going about his duties, was conked on the side of the head by one of the small wooden mugs that was on a shelf behind him just above the liquor bottles. The staff would set the tables in the dining room before closing the doors for the evening. When the doors were unlocked the next day, the napkins and silverware were often found in disarray or on the floor, as if someone was not happy with the arrangement of the settings. A guest staying in room 7 was disturbed from his slumber several times by his door opening and closing with no visible hands to cause the motion. Bottles being knocked over and moans heard from the basement are other common haunts of the inn.

Salem author Robert Ellis Cahill and a few of his friends once booked an overnight stay at the inn. Although he experienced nothing unusual, his friend in another room claimed to have been bothered all night by an unearthly moaning.

One day, a woman named Priscilla Perkins Kenney came to the inn after reading an article in the paper about Cyrus. She began reminiscing about her father, Silas Perkins, who worked at the inn for eight years up until his death. The names Cyrus and Silas were too close for coincidence. Mr. Perkins was an acknowledged poet in Kennebunk and Kennebunkport. His work was published in major newspapers, and one of his poems, "The Common Road," was broadcast over national hookup from President Franklin D. Roosevelt's funeral train.

Silas worked at the Kennebunk Inn as a night watchman and clerk. He would spend the long hours of silence in the basement writing his verses. In June 1952, seventy-two-year-old Silas Perkins strolled out of the inn to buy a newspaper. His heart gave out, and he was carried back to the inn, where he died in the Fireplace Room, presently also known as room 11. His permanent status at the inn still seems to continue, as Mr. Perkins refuses to give up his position as part of the staff.

Our tenure at the inn had a few minor but notable occurrences. The dresser in the room had a handle that would rap against the drawer if you walked by it. Being next to the main part of the floor, this was constant. Later in the waning hours of the night, we were awoken several times by the rapping of the handle and the creaking of the floorboards at the foot of the bed. I attributed the incidents to be possible vibrations caused by the flow of traffic along the main road. At one point, I got up to get some water and was accosted by a chilling cold spot just past the bed near the radiator, which was piping hot. Other than that, our photographs showed no strange anomalies, and all instrument and tape recordings turned up nothing else unusual. I even politely asked Silas if he wanted to talk while we were recording, but I guess he was as tired as we were that night.

A few employees had some tales to share of napkins being lifted and dropped by unseen hands and footsteps ascending the stairs from an invisible source even when they are watching the staircase. Activity in the bar is still a thrill to patrons either stopping to wet their whistle or partake in one of the delicious selections from the kitchen. The sounds of someone walking around in empty rooms are a regular part of the enchantment of the inn.

My wife and I returned to the inn in the late spring of 2005 to get an update on the haunted happenings at the Kennebunk. We talked to the new bartender and a few staff members. The staff claimed that some still hear old Silas making his nightly rounds in the otherwise empty bedchambers upstairs, particularly room 11. The bar was still somewhat active with spirit activity, but not as frequent as before. Maybe Silas has moved upstairs to fulfill his tenure or is just feeling a little complacent.

Since then, we have been back several times. Each visit, staff and patrons have stories to tell. The inn's website characterizes the paranormal phenomena as a distinctive feature. It is not celebrating a mischievous haunting as much as embracing the energy that the inn exudes. The more modern renovations to the Kennebunk have enhanced its charm without taking away from its historical value. The inn's restaurant serves wonderful food and spirits. Perhaps Silas feels forever at home in the place that is so accommodating to its guests.

Spend a night and you might find out yourself if he is permanently checked in at the Kennebunk Inn.

A Cemetery with No Bodies?

I have heard this story from several sources who appear to be reliable, living as they do within the region where this next story takes place. The town of Litchfield, New Hampshire, is located along the banks of the Merrimack River. The river stretches and winds its way from the juncture of the Pemigewasset and Winnipesaukee Rivers in New Hampshire 117 miles to its mouth in Newburyport, Massachusetts. Its name is said to mean "place of strong current." This would only stand to validate the legend that is now at your perusal. There is a section along Route 3A in Litchfield where the great river bottlenecks. This is the site of Litchfield's first meetinghouse. The meetinghouse was established in 1740 and was discontinued in 1899. There is a stone monument along the bank of the river on the site of the former house of worship.

The areas along the Merrimack River have endured many floods over the centuries. The first documented flood in the Granite State was recorded in December 1740 when the Merrimack River spilled over its banks onto the land around it. This would be a common occurrence for centuries to come.

Along with the church sat the village burial ground, laid out along the banks of the river. In the early 1800s, there was a terrible flood that washed away the caskets and bodies of the cemetery. Records show two floods that were disastrous to the vicinity, one in 1847 and one in 1852. The townspeople recovered some of the heavier stones. According to the legend, town officials moved those stones across the street behind the new church. The lost markers were re-created from memory and existing family monuments.

Monument on the Merrimack River in Litchfield, New Hampshire, commemorating the site of the town's first meetinghouse.

Litchfield's "Cemetery with No Bodies" looks like the legend could have some truth behind it as the stones all look similar and are so close together.

This is why many of the markers look exactly alike despite the difference in years. The fact that many of them are so close together is also a conclusive deduction that no one is interred under most of the stones. Although the dead do not rest there, it is reported that they do seem to reside in the graveyard, for there is a great amount of energy floating around the stones. Investigators have recorded voices within the cemetery. Some were not so cordial, while others were benevolent. One theory is that the few interred within the cemetery are in search of their loved ones. Another is that those who were once buried near the river remain in spirit and are eternally searching for their mortal remains. This legend is just a short anecdote to pass a few moments, but it remains quite an interesting tale. It makes you wonder how much of it is fact and how much of the story is missing. It can be assumed that there have to be some interments in the cemetery, as people who died in the preceding years would most likely be buried there. That would make it a cemetery with *some* bodies, unless the legend holds true to its name. But then again, just because there may be no bodies does not mean that there is nobody there.

THE SACO RIVER'S UNDYING CURSE

Even the story proclaiming the origin of this magnificent 136-mile waterway is steeped in magic and legend. The Saco River originates from Saco Lake at Crawford Notch in the White Mountains, descending 1,500 feet as it flows through Hart's Location, Bartlett and Conway before entering Maine. The river eventually flows into the Atlantic Ocean at Ferry Beach, where the twin cities of Saco and Biddeford are located.

The creation of the Saco, according to Charles Skinner's book *Myths and Legends of Our Land*, credits the mighty waterway to the manitou named Glooskap:

> *Water-Goblins from the streams about Katahdin had left their birthplace and journeyed away to the Agiochooks, making their presence known to the Indians of that region by thefts and loss of life. When the manitou, Glooskap, learned that these goblins were eating human flesh and committing other outrages, he took on their own form, turning half his body into stone, and went in search of them. The wigwam had been pitched near the Home of the Water Fairies—a name absurdly changed by the people of North Conway to Diana's Bath—and on entering he was invited to take meat. The tail of a whale was cooked and offered to him, but after he had taken it upon his knees one of the goblins exclaimed, "That is too good for a beggar like you," and snatched it away. Glooskap had merely to wish the return of the dainty when it flew back into his platter. Then he took the whale's jaw, and snapped it like a reed; he filled his pipe and burned the tobacco to ashes*

in one inhalation; when his hosts closed the wigwam and smoked vigorously, intending to foul the air and stupefy him, he enjoyed it, while they grew sick; so they whispered to each other, "This is a mighty magician, and we must try his powers in another way."

A game of ball was proposed, and, adjourning to a sandy level at the bend of the Saco, they began to play, but Glooskap found that the ball was a hideous skull that rolled and snapped at him and would have torn his flesh had it not been immortal and immovable from his bones. He crushed it at a blow, and breaking off the bough of a tree he turned it by a word into a skull ten times larger than the other that flew after the wicked people as a wildcat leaps upon a rabbit. Then the god stamped on the sands and all the springs were opened in the mountains, so that the Saco came rising through the valley with a roar that made the nations tremble. The goblins were caught in the flood and swept into the sea, where Glooskap changed them into fish.

Arlene's daughter, Mandy, lives in Biddeford, so we have visited the area on countless occasions. In fact, we frequently find ourselves on what is now known as Factory Island and was once called Indian Island. This is where the story of one of the longest-lasting curses in New England was born—a curse that has lingered for more than three centuries. Of course, over the centuries, the legend has become convoluted or just plain transformed with various adaptations to suit the storyteller. But there are enough similarities in the various versions to get the point across of why mothers would not allow their children to wade in the river.

The Sokoki tribe was a subdivision of the Abenaki (actually Wabanaki, "those living at the sunrise, or east") nation, living near the mouth of the Saco River. Their sagamore, Squando, was not only a young, strong, well-known and respected chief but also a mighty shaman whose mysterious powers commanded great reverence from his followers. The Sokokis lived in harmony with the white settlers of the area. In fact, it is told that Squando once rescued a young white girl from captivity and returned her to her family as a gesture of friendship and peace. According to the history of Saco and Biddeford, after a defeat during King Philip's War, Squando returned captives, including one woman named Elizabeth Wakely, taken at Casco. She was returned in June 1676 to Major Waldron as a gesture of peace, which was once again restored until August of the same year. Let's step back a bit and tell the legend from the beginning.

When it came time to choose a wife, Squando was very particular and chose a beautiful woman named Awagimiska. The two soon had a son named Mikoudou. His father could not be more proud of the young brave, who would someday lead his people. He became even more elated when he found that his wife was once again with child.

The year was 1675, and the colonies were deep in the throes of King Philip's War, one of the bloodiest wars ever fought on American soil. The Sokokis, however, stayed neutral, staying at peace with their neighbors. One day, the pregnant Awagimiska rowed from Indian Island, with Mikoudou wrapped in a blanket. Three Englishmen had rowed upriver after mooring their ship at the mouth of the Saco. When they spied the woman and her baby, they joked to one another, saying something to the effect of, "I have heard that Indian babies can swim naturally from birth much like brute animals."

One of the men convinced the other two that they should test the assertion. The three rowed their boat to Awagimiska's canoe and proceeded to wrestle with the boat until it tipped over, spilling all inhabitants into the river. Another version tells that one of the men wrenched the baby from the woman's arms and flung it into the rushing river. Awagimiska broke free from the men and dove into the water to save her drowning baby. Whether they were surprised that the young Indian did not float is not recorded. The three men rowed off and soon forgot about the incident. Awagimiska recovered her baby, but the child never recovered from the ordeal and died a few days later.

When the chief heard of the incident, he became violently outraged. Wading into the quickening flow of the river, Squando held his arms toward the heavens and, summoning all his powers of magic, screamed a curse on the white man that the river shall forever claim three of his kind every year. He then used his powers of authority to rally his tribe in siding with King Philip in the war against the colonies by uniting Androscoggin warriors in his cause. They raided colonial villages with vengeance and fire in their eyes, driving out as many settlers as they could.

In case you are wondering how the situation ended, a treaty was signed in Cocheco on September 6 and in Boston on November 6, 1676. More terms were agreed on at Casco Bay in 1678 with Squando and other chiefs. One of the stipulations for peace was that the inhabitants could return to their homes but had to forfeit one peck of corn from every household annually by way of acknowledgement to the Indians for possession of their land. Oh, and here's another little secret: Squando, if he lived on the island, shared it with a white man. In 1667, Major William Phillips conveyed half of the island to Captain John Bonython in consideration of eight hundred pine trees for merchantable boards. This took place eight years before the war and curse that would plague the white men.

Factory Island in Saco-Biddeford looks nothing like it did when Squando resided there. This view shows the only section of the island that is not cramped with massive mills. Note the two smokestacks in the background.

The treaty, although it reestablished coexistence between the two cultures, did not lift the curse bestowed on the white men by Squando. Every year since that fateful day, the river has claimed its bounty, sometimes even more than necessary needed to satisfy the curse. People who lived near the river or knew of the curse stayed clear of the foreboding banks until the waterway had claimed its three lives. In 1947, the headline of the *Maine Sunday Telegram* joyously proclaimed, "Saco River Outlives Curse of Indian Chief." It was the first recorded time that the mighty Saco had not bent to the curse, as there were no known fatalities from the river reported that year. This has not stopped the curse from holding a fearful grip on those who dare defy the famous words of an angry chief. Arlene's daughter, Mandy, who lives in Biddeford, just before the Saco line, attests that since she moved there, the river has taken at least one life per year. Maybe the curse has dwindled in strength over the centuries, or perhaps the vengeful spirit of Squando has become somewhat forgiving with the passing of time. Still, the Saco River brings woe to those who are not careful or respectful, and the foreboding legacy of its past cannot be denied, especially the curse that has lasted for centuries.

New England's Only Stigmatist

Marie Rose Ferron represents the only known case of stigmata in New England history. Stigmata are the appearance of marks on the body resembling those of Christ at the time he was crucified. History has recorded few cases of stigmata and even fewer that exhibit all of the wounds Jesus received during his persecution. "Little Rose," as she was called, was documented to have exhibited all five: the marks of the thorns around her head, the lance wound in her side, the four marks from being nailed to the cross, a shoulder wound and bleeding from the eyes.

Marie Rose, daughter of Jean-Baptiste and Delima Ferron, was born in Quebec, Canada, on May 24, 1902, in a stable, like Jesus, across from the home in which the family lived. Mrs. Ferron had gone out to tend to the animals when she began hemorrhaging, forcing her to give birth to Rose in the stable. She was one of fifteen children who would be taught the rosary. It is said that Mrs. Ferron's giving birth to fifteen children symbolized the fifteen mysteries of the rosary. Rose, being the tenth child, symbolized the tenth mystery, the mystery of crucifixion. Rose was about four and a half years old when the family left the Saint-Germain-de-Grantham province of Quebec to live in the United States, finally moving to Woonsocket, where Rose would spend the rest of her days before her death on May 11, 1936.

Although she was born with a rare, crippling form of arthritis, she still carried herself with a sense of joy and keen wit. At an early age, she exhibited uncanny abilities. She would pray to St. Anthony to find lost items. Mr. Ferron was a blacksmith by trade. He loved his family and would play the violin and have the children sing and dance. He once hid his shoes in a place he was sure Rose could not find them and asked her to get his shoes for him. She wandered out of the house and past the train tracks, right to where he had so carefully hidden them from watchful eyes.

It was around this time that she began to have visions and periods of ecstasy during which it was reported she communicated with Jesus. This happened with startling regularity. Rose, at age twelve, decided to help the family by working as a nursemaid while they lived in Fall River, Massachusetts, before moving to Woonsocket, Rhode Island. During this time, she experienced her first battles with sickness. One morning, after having a fever, her right hand and foot became paralyzed to the point that she needed crutches to move about. Two years later, after a blessing of holy water, her hand that had been closed since the fever slowly opened and was restored. Her foot never healed, and in time, the other foot would become lame as well.

By the time Rose was seventeen, she was suffering with arthritis to the point that even the use of crutches was painful. Rose was twenty-three years old when the family moved to Woonsocket. By this time, she was mostly bedridden. Still, her healing powers reached far beyond her physical restrictions.

Her sister Florema, widowed with seven children, was stricken with a cerebral hemorrhage, incapacitating her left arm to the point where she could not work to help support her children. Rose promised her that by the end of the week, she would have use of it again. On Thursday of that same week, the left hand was completely healed. She quickly called on Rose to tell her of the miracle but learned that Rose's left hand had become paralyzed that same day. Florema begged Rose to take back her gift, but Little Rose refused, stating that she had no need for her hand, being an invalid.

In 1926, Rose began having occasions of stigmata. During Lent of 1927, the wounds began to appear regularly. Red and purple stripes appeared on her arm, resembling the lashes of whips. The wounds swelled and hurt like burns. On Fridays, Rose would suffer the "passion." Her wounds would open, and large quantities of blood would flow from them. Her mother continually wrapped bandages around the wounds and covered the bed in towels. By Saturday, the only sign of the wounds were small marks on her skin. These events were often photographed regularly, solidifying her passions as one of the most well-documented cases of stigmata in history.

Marie Rose Ferron died in 1936 at the age of thirty-three, the same age as Christ when he was crucified. She was buried at Precious Blood Cemetery in Woonsocket. Her grave is about two hundred feet in, along the right-hand road at the first intersection. After her death, she was exhumed for

The grave site of Marie Rose Ferron, New England's only stigmattee, at
Precious Blood Cemetery, Woonsocket, Rhode Island.

further proof of stigmata. Tests were deemed conclusive. A few applications
for sainthood have been denied. Some contend that the reason was more
political than pious. She still seems to heal from the grave to this very day.
Scores of religious pilgrims flock to her simple stone to absorb the healing
energy said to radiate from her burial plot.

THE MAGIC OF THE EDDYS

S even miles north of Rutland, Vermont, in a wooded valley shut in by the slopes of the beautiful Green Mountains and lying high above the tidewater, is the tiny hamlet of Chittenden. On a quiet back road, not far from this little community and facing away from the road, sits a large, remodeled nineteenth-century farmhouse. The building is now a ski lodge in the possession of the High Life Ski Club, but it was once the center of communication with the spirit universe.

An attorney and former Civil War colonel, Henry Steel Olcott (August 2, 1832–February 17, 1907), while writing for the *New York Sun*, paid a ten-week visit to the Eddy family to find out once and for all if what he had heard was actually true; allegedly, the members of the Eddy family possessed an incredible supernatural ability to summon the dead. The Spiritual movement was at its height around 1874, and there were many who claimed to have the same uncanny powers that defied logic and reason. Very few, if any, would leave a lasting impression on those who witnessed these "acts" of mediumship such as the Eddy family claimed to possess. Many writings focus on two members, William and Horatio, but it is known that most of the eleven children had amazing powers inherited from their mother's ancestry. Olcott published his experience with the Eddy family in his book *People from the Other World* in 1874, giving us the most complete perspsective of what happened at the Eddy homestead before and during his tenure there.

Zephaniah Eddy and his wife, Julia Ann MacCombs, had eleven known children: John Westley (born in 1832), William H. (1832–October 25, 1932),

Francis Lightfoot (1834–March 18, 1862), Maranda D. (1836–March 29, 1871), Sophia Jane (February 2, 1840–July 18, 1913), Horatio G. (1842–September 8, 1922), Mary C. (April 1, 1844–December 31, 1910), James H. (1846–April 18, 1862), Delia M. (1849–January 28, 1922, although her stone states her birthdate as 1853), Daniel Webster (September 17, 1852–September 6, 1926) and Alice Julia (April 2, 1857–April 20, 1887).

All of them exhibited strange powers beyond rational explanation. Their mother, Julia, came from a long line of mediums and psychics. Her great-great-grandmother, Mary Perkins Bradbury, was tried, convicted and sentenced to hang on September 22, 1692, for witchcraft during the Salem witch hysteria. Somehow, perhaps due to a bribe for the jailer or a daring escape, she managed to gain freedom and flee to Amesbury. After the hysteria had dwindled, she returned to Salisbury, where she died on December 20, 1700.

Zephaniah, being ill educated, close-minded and perhaps fearful of that which he did not understand, often chastised his wife for exhibiting her uncanny ability in any form. Of course, she could not always control her gift, and this sometimes led to physical restraint by her husband. This was especially true when they began having children. Ethereal voices rang throughout the home, pounding and banging would shake the structure and the children were often levitated from their cribs by unseen hands and found in various places throughout the Eddy homestead. These forms of spirit activity would later carry over to the children.

Often they would be seen playing in the fields, and suddenly other children would appear out of nowhere, romping around with the young Eddys. When Zephaniah approached these children, the spirits would vanish. They seemed to appear at random and move items to and fro about the home. This was most disconcerting to Mr. Eddy and led to many beatings of the children. These strange occurences followed them to school, where desks levitated and quills, inkwell, books and slates flew about the room whenever the Eddy boys were in the classroom. Because of this, William and Horatio grew up illiterate, having been deprived of a basic education. Mrs. Eddy knew how to control her gifts for the most part, but the children had no idea what was happening most of the time. Of all the children, Maranda was the most gifted.

Maranda at one point began to see her brothers James and Francis, who had died in 1862. They told her that she was going to join them shortly. Knowing that she had little time left in her mortal frame, Maranda requested a special epitaph be carved into her tombstone that read, "Not dead but risen. Why seek ye the living among the dead." The second sentence of the epitaph is taken from Luke 24:5 in the King James version of the Holy Bible: "And as they were afraid, and bowed down their faces to the earth, they said unto them, why seek ye the living among the dead?" The first sentence could also have been a revised wording borrowed from a section of Luke 24:6: "He is not here, but is risen."

Mrs. Stephen Baird comforted Maranda during her last hours on the day of March 29, 1871, and was there to hold her when she gave her last breath. Then something astonishing happened. Here is what Mary Baird wrote in regard to the account: "Chittenden, October 5, 1874—I certify that I was present on the occasion of Maranda Eddy's death; that I held her up at the last moment; and that, just at her last gasp, her arm rose and her right hand closed her eyes."

There was always a strange, ethereal occurrence before each member of the Eddy family passed on. One evening, a beautiful, ornate coach pulled into the front yard. The driver, dressed in fine clothing, sat there as did a woman, who was attired in exquisite Scotch plaid and furs. The two appeared to be European in manner and dress. The woman bowed silently before some Eddy boys and then slowly faded away. The boys grabbed a lantern and searched the road and yard for carriage tracks but found none. A few months later, their grandmother, Lydia MacCombs, passed away. She was of Scotch ancestry.

The boys slept on the second floor in the north room, where a spinning wheel was located. Soon after their grandmother's death, the wheel began to turn while they slept, waking them in a most frightful manner. It was soon learned that grandmother MacCombs's ghost was returning in the night to do her spinning, as slowly, over time, her form became more and more distinct with each appearance. The boys were relieved by this and hung a bell on the wheel that would ring and wake them when she made her nightly visit.

Mrs. Eddy passed away in 1872 after a long illness. During her infirmity, spirits often materialized in her room. One in particular, her deceased daughter Maranda, came back from beyond the veil to comfort and care for her dying mother. Just before Mrs. Eddy passed, her mother, Mrs. MacCombs, appeared, telling the family that her daughter would soon pass over the river to her.

Francis Lightfoot Eddy served as orderly sergeant of Company G, 5th Vermont Volunteers. During this time, he took ill with a cold. This cold eventually turned into consumption, thus sealing his fate. Francis, working on a vision he experienced, penned a notation in the family Bible stating the exact time and date he would die. One evening, the sound of a wagon came to a halt in front of the Eddys' door. The family then heard some scuffling, and the front door opened to reveal two soldiers carrying a coffin with a brass nameplate on the lid. The soldiers uttered not a single sound as they solemnly lowered the coffin to the floor and exited.

The dim light of the hallway made it difficult to read the name on the plate. The family quickly dispersed in search of a candle to illuminate the plate. Upon returning, they found that the coffin had vanished. Francis passed on to the other side on March 18, 1862, at the age of twenty-eight. The family ordered a coffin from nearby Rutland. Imagine their surprise when the coffin that was unloaded from the delivery wagon was the exact one that the ghostly soldiers had brought a short time before, complete with nameplate. Francis had an inscription carved into his stone that read, "Passed into the world of spirits." This verse, or something like it, would become a common inscription on several of the Eddy gravestones. "Entered the world of spirits" is inscribed on Julia and Maranda's stone, who died in 1871 and 1872, respectively. "Passed to spirit life" can be found on the monuments of William, Horatio, Alice and a few others who were immediate relations of the family. Incidently, Francis's brother James died exactly one month later on April 18. Their father followed them on July 13 of the same year.

As stated before, Mr. Eddy often resorted to physical restraint when it came to the children exhibiting their gifts. William once fell into a deep trance, and all efforts to wake him failed. Mr. Eddy angrily began to prod and pinch him, at one point resorting to physical blows in an attempt to wake his son. When this failed to bring William around, a neighbor, Anson Ladd, with the father's permission, poured scalding water down the young fellow's back and then placed a red-hot ember from the fireplace on his head. The two extreme acts did nothing to stir William, although the physical scars of these actions stayed with him the rest of his life.

When Mr. Eddy realized that his children were not going to stop their inevitable displays of mediumship and telepathy, he came up with an alternative idea. In 1847, he sent four of the children off to be put on show for profit. For the next fourteen years, the show toured every major city in the country and even made a stop in London. While Mr. Eddy reaped the benefits of their gifts, the children were tested and tortured in countless ways in attempts to disprove their authenticity as mediums. They were bound in contorted positions, had wax poured over their lips, were tied to beds and were placed in various other conditions by skeptics that left scars and bone damage on their bodies.

The Eddy Plot in Baird Cemetery near the family's former home in Chittenden, Vermont.

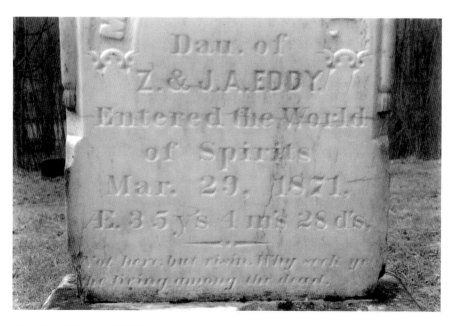

Epitaph on Maranda Eddy's stone reads, "Not here but risen. Why seek ye the living among the dead."

They were mobbed in several cities that were less tolerant of their "acts of the devil." In south Danvers, Massachusetts, they were shot at by the locals. William received a bullet wound to the ankle and Mary one to her arm, while Horatio was stabbed in the leg. In west Cleveland, Ohio, William was ridden out on rails and luckily escaped being tarred and feathered. In Lynn, Massachusetts, Horatio was hit with a brick in the forehead and suffered a broken finger. These are just a sample of the horrors the children endured at the hands of those who were skeptical of their powers. As far as anyone knows, no one was ever able to disprove their abilities.

If the dates serve correctly, William was fifteen years old in 1847. Horatio would have been five years old, Maranda eleven, Sophia seven and Mary only three or four years old.

Years later, at their home in Chittenden, the now adult brothers William and Horatio began holding circles of mediumship for spectators in a special room constructed specifically for that purpose. They opened their doors as the Green Tavern, taking in visitors to witness their shows. Six days a week, William would enter a small cabinet in the right corner of the circle room and fall into a deep trance. Then various spirits would emerge from the box, singing, dancing and speaking to the crowd. Among them were William's mother, an Indian woman named Honto, several deceased neighbors and children and even deceased loved ones of the spectators who, in many cases, were unknown to the Eddy family.

Mr. Olcott arrived at the Eddy home on September 17, 1874, and attended a circle that very evening. The circles had become regular presentations at the home just one month before. Twenty-five people were assembled in the room, many from out of town, to see the Eddy brothers exhibit their otherworldly talents. William entered the spirit cabinet, and shortly afterward, music began to play, yet there were no devices to create the sounds that filled the chamber. Within a few minutes, the voice of an old woman rang out from behind the curtain that hung over the door of the cabinet.

At first, there were murmurs of trickery, but when the spirit of a neighbor, Mrs. Eaton, manifested in front of the throng, all doubts were extinguished. Honto was next. She was young, with a dark complexion, and stood about five feet, three inches tall. Someone suggested that a neighbor and spectator, Mrs. Cleveland, check the beating of Honto's heart to prove that she was real and not an image somehow illuminated through lights and mirrors. Mrs. Cleveland put her hand on Honto's chest. Her flesh was moist and cold, and there was a faint but definite heartbeat. Her wrists also produced a pulse.

The famous Eddy house in Chittenden, Vermont, is now home to the High Life Ski Club.

Mr. Olcott, being an avid investigator, noted very carefully all of her traits and physical demeanor during the ten weeks he witnessed the Eddy séances. Honto, along with most of the four hundred different spirits that emerged from the cabinet during his stay, bore no physical resemblance to William in any way. Close examination of the cabinet and the room proved that there was no obvious form of trickery used. The cabinet was barely large enough to fit William, let alone a whole troupe of actors and the various garments they wore.

Two more Indian women of different appearance and dress emerged from the cabinet, the latter dancing and playing violin. Mr. Olcott witnessed during his stay that William was neither musically inclined nor had any grace whatsoever when it came to dancing, as there were dances occasionally held before the circles would commence. Several more spirits emerged from the cabinet that evening, none of them physically resembling William. Among them were a six-foot-three Indian named Santum and William H. Reynolds of the Reynolds Brothers Shoe Manufacturing in Utica, New York, who died on May 6 that same year of a fever. His brother John, who passed on November 15, 1860, also appeared. George Reynolds, the surviving sibling, was present in the crowd to witness their emergence from the cabinet but

The graves of brothers William and Horatio Eddy at Chittenden, Vermont's Horton Cemetery.

was aghast when his fifteen-year-old deceased nephew, Stephen Hopkins, threw aside the curtain and made his entrance on the small platform in front of the crowd. Mr. George Brown, the late father of Edward Brown, Delia Eddy's husband, also appeared before the crowd.

During Olcott's lengthy stay, he witnessed and recorded more than four hundred different spirits and collected hundreds of affidavits and testimony by those who witnessed these amazing events. Carpenters and other various tradesmen examined the house from top to bottom with Olcott and could not come up with a single solitary inch of the place where trickery or fraud may have been instituted. The astute investigator left no stone unturned in his investigation and yet could not explain what transpired before his and other witnesses' eyes night after night.

Eventually, fights and arguments between William, Horatio and Mary spelled the end of the circles. Mary and her family moved to Pittsford, where she became a full-time medium, Horatio moved into a house across the street and took to gardening, part-time mediumship and parlor tricks for the local children, while William stayed in the family home. Horatio married Thelma Hussey on September 22, 1886. As far as is known, they had no children. William married twice, the first marriage to Sarah Drown on December 14, 1870, and the second to Alice Parent on January 1, 1889. Neither marriage produced any offspring. Mary married Hiram Judson Huntoon on July 4, 1868, and had three children. Mary passed away on December 31, 1910, in Rutland and is buried at the East Pittsford Cemetery. Horatio died on September 8, 1922. William passed on October 25, 1932, at the age of ninety-nine. Both are interred at the Horton Cemetery in Chittenden along with Sophia. The rest of the family members, save Delia, are buried in the Eddy lot within the confines of the Baird Cemetery in Chittenden. An interesting note: a letter written by Horatio Eddy in July 1878 was published in the *Boston Investigator* (1831–1904). Horatio declared his sister, Mary Huntoon, to be a fraud and his brother William "no better than she is, and a thorough exposure of their tricks would be just and right."

Horatio wrote to Mrs. Margaret Flint, a woman who was present when Mary was accused of trickery during a séance in Webster, Massachusetts. Mrs. Flint forwarded the following letter to the newspaper for print.

Chittenden (Vt.), July 29, 1878.

MRS. FLINT:

Although an entire stranger to you, allow me to write you a few lines in regard to Mrs. Huntoon, my sister. When she was at your place I believed her then to be an honest medium, and the story she told on her arrival of her abuse by you. Then I had some sympathy for her. But since that time I have become fully satisfied she was thoroughly exposed in some of her meanness at your place, and when I found all her statements were false concerning you and your family, I informed her of it. Since that time she has tried many plots to ruin me. One in last September. She and her husband, who is one of the biggest scoundrels that ever run, went to the State Attorney and entered a complaint against me for an assault upon them with intent to kill, and the result was, that by her and her false swearing I am bound over to this coming September Court for trial, which is one of the vilest games that could be got up, and all for a revengeful purpose.

Now she and her husband, I learn, are going to Lake Pleasant Camp meeting to defraud the people there, and get money to carry out some of their fiendish plans. If she could be thoroughly exposed there in one of her first seances, and arrested for obtaining money under false pretences, it would put an end to her career in that line, and as you have become aware that she is a fraud, you could do it easier than anyone else. Her brother, Wm. Eddy, may be with her ; if so, he is not better than she is, and a thorough exposure of their tricks would be just and right. She has told many stories in regard to your character which I have found to be false, and if I am her brother, I will say to you that she is one of the meanest persons that ever existed, and her husband is just as mean as she is—nothing too mean for them to do for a dollar ; and as friend to you for showing them up in the past, I would inquire if there is not some way they can be brought to justice ? I should like to have a long talk with you, but as I am situated I shall have to give it up. Could you send me the letter that was published in the Boston paper by you, where she claimed her arm was broken ? It may be of some use for me in the coming trial—showing she was a liar. Anything you can do to help me in my trouble by her false complaint, will in the future be made up by me if possible.

HORATIO G. EDDY.

After Mary's exposure, it appears she took much offense to the Flints and began a campaign to discredit their findings. It also appears that the Eddy family actually had a falling out of some sort, creating much discord between Horatio and his brother and sister. Still, we have only a few cases of trickery versus the many who verified the authenticity of the Eddys' abilities.

"It may be said that the Eddys' took what they knew to the grave but it is more aptly put that they also took what they knew of the grave with them to the living."

Before his stay in Chittenden, Olcott was not an enthusiast of the Spiritualist movement. His time spent at the Eddy home forever changed his way of thinking in regard to the spirit world. In 1875, together with Helena P. Blavatsky (whom he had met during his visit to the Eddy home) and William Q. Judge, Olcott cofounded the Theosophical Society and remained president-founder for life.

The Devil in New England

The devil has certainly left his impression on New England in more ways than one. Between pacts, places bearing his moniker and scores of marks left etched in rocks, the dark one has been very busy over the centuries trying to recruit the folks of the region to his side. The following stories are but a drop in the bucket compared to the amount of influence the devil has had on New England and its people. Some will be familiar, while others will be more obscure. They are in no particular order, so there is not one favorite tale or specific length that will be especially addressed. Enjoy.

There are two Purgatory Chasms in southern New England. One is located in Sutton, Massachusetts, while the other can be seen in Middletown, Rhode Island. People often get them confused and tend to mix up the legends as well. The Sutton chasm is a quarter-mile crevice, with cliffs towering seventy feet above the floor. There are several trails that run around and through the notch where places like Devil's Pulpit, Devil's Coffin and Devil's Corncrib entice the more daring to either climb or crawl through these natural crevices and creations.

According to the legend I heard, a brave Indian sought the hand of a beautiful Indian woman. They courted for a short time, and being head over heels for her, he told her he would do anything for her hand in marriage. The woman, being selfish and vain as well as beautiful, told the brave that she would have him if he could jump the width of the crevice, landing safely on the other side. The brave then realized his foolishness in wanting such a selfish woman for beauty alone. He summoned all his strength and, with a great bounding leap, cleared the giant hole and kept on running, leaving the woman by herself. Hobomocko, the Indian version of the devil, then appeared and took her away as punishment for requesting such a deed. I have also heard this for the next chasm as well.

Purgatory Chasm in Middletown, Rhode Island, is a fifty-foot crevice dropping 160 feet into the ocean. Legend has it that an Indian woman murdered a white man, and Hobomocko whisked her to the chasm, where he tried to make his move on her. When she resisted, he banged her head against the rocks, creating the bowl-like impressions in the boulder. He then swung his great hatchet at her. Missing her, he cracked the ledge in two, creating the great chasm. He then grabbed her and, with the fury of hell, ran with her toward the edge of the cliff, burning his footprints into the stone. At the edge, he lopped off her head and threw her into the sea. Another version has Hobomocko also cursing her headless ghost to wander the nearby beach, eternally searching for her head.

While we are on the subject of Purgatory Chasm in Middletown, there is a story concerning Devil's Foot Rock in nearby North Kingstown. I have heard two stories regarding the footprints in the rock. Here is a relation of both accounts. The first involves a beautiful Indian maiden who was walking along the old Route 1 alongside the edifice. A stranger dressed in a long black cape and hat came upon her and began to flirt with her. His advances went unanswered. Finally, in a fit of anger, he thrust back his cape and lifted his hat, revealing that he was Hobomocko. He then swooped up the young maiden and, with several bounds, leapt into the air carrying the woman away toward Purgatory Chasm in Middletown. While bounding for takeoff, his cloven hoofs left small craters in the ledge that are still visible to this day. This story is also sometimes associated with Purgatory Chasm itself.

The other version concerns Reverend Samuel Nickles of Providence, who was on his way home on old Route 1 in Wickford after giving a sermon. The rain began to fall hard and heavy as he prodded forth on his trusty nag. He lowered his head to the rain, pulling up the collar of his coat over him to keep dry. All of a sudden, there was a rumbling of the earth. When the good reverend looked up, he saw the devil's incarnation of Peter Rugg, the ghostly rider who haunts the roads of New England, and his Roman-nosed bay bearing down on him. Flames shot from the horse's eyes and mouth as he raced toward the priest at a furious clip. Reverend Nickles's horse shied back, throwing the minister onto the back of the fiery steed. The reverend screamed and held on for his life as the horse bolted up the rocky ledge that laced the side of the road. The reverend was then thrown from the fiery beast.

Purgatory Chasm in Middletown is a favorite attraction. This is where Hobomocko created the crevice with his axe before beheading a woman and throwing her over the ledge.

Devil's Foot Rock along the old Route 1 in South Kingstown, Rhode Island, where the devil's footprints are easily seen burned into the top of the ledge.

When the pastor came to, the sun was shining, and there was his nag, Romeo, feeding on grass by the road. Reverend Nickles gazed at the rock in disbelief. Burned into the rock ledge were cloven hoof prints left by the devil horse where it had dashed up the rock. For years to come, Reverend Nickles would give sermons at the rock where he once encountered the devil's incarnate of Peter Rugg and his horse.

Chapman Falls in East Haddam is located in Devil's Hopyard State Park. It is long told that the devil would sit on the ledge at the top of the falls, with his serpent tongued tail slung over his shoulder, and play his golden violin for the witches who stirred their wicked brews in the glacial potholes along the falls. How it became known as Devil's Hopyard concerns a legend of a man named Dibble, who grew hops along the Eight Mile River. He would use these hops for his strong liquor, which the younger generation of the village frequently imbibed. Many of his parties usually got out of control due to the excessive drinking from his tubs of intemperance. One local mother once found her son drunk beyond reason from Dibble's moonshine and cursed the man for making the "devil's drink." She convinced many of her neighbors that Dibble was in league with Satan, out to destroy the chastity of their kinfolk. Over time, that cursing and cussing of Dibble's hopyard sort of twisted the name into Devil's Hopyard.

In Montville, Connecticut, there is a footprint left by the devil near the Mohegan Church. Tradition has it that when the dark one decided to depart Shelter Island, he took three bounding leaps—the first was on the island, the second on Orient Point and the third on Montauk—before plunging into the briny deep. The cloven hoof print is still visible to this day.

The devil has also left his name in the history books of Norton, Massachusetts. Major George Leonard, a member of one of the prominent families of Norton during the seventeenth and eighteenth centuries, wished for wealth and power. His father was a well-respected minister in the area, and the devil was all too happy to grant George his wish. The dark one gave the usual pitch and then produced a pen and parchment, whereupon George agreeably signed his name.

In 1695, at the age of twenty-five, George married Anna Tisdale and became exceedingly wealthy, owning one of the largest estates in the region. Leonard Mansion became the pride of Norton, but that was to be short-lived. Although the devil promised George that he would be well off for the rest of his life, he did not specify how long that life would be. George died in 1716 at the age of forty-six.

In keeping with the customs of the day, George was laid out upstairs, while family and friends grieved his passing downstairs. Suddenly, a terrible clamor arose from above, and the mourners rushed upstairs to investigate the source of the disruption. Anna, being the first to bolt up the stairs, threw open the door to the room where George lay and came face to face with the Prince of Darkness, eyes blazing red, scowling with a sinister chuckle. Without hesitation, he grabbed George Leonard's body and leaped out the window. The devil landed on a boulder below the window, searing his hoof print into the rock before bounding off into oblivion with Leonard tucked under his arm. As his laughter faded into the night, Anna noticed the blood-signed parchment floating gently to the floor. She picked it up and threw it into the fireplace, where it burst immediately into flames. The next day, the family noticed the imprint that the devil had made in the rock. George Leonard's son and grandson would both go on to become lawyers and judges. Hmmm.

The "devil's darning needle" is an old nickname for a dragonfly. It was believed that if one landed on your head, it would tangle your hair so badly that you would have no other choice but to cut it off. Then there is the old tale we heard as children that if a dragonfly (or "sewing needle," as we called it) flew too close to your face, it would sew your lips shut so tight that you would never again be able to separate them. This is believed to be on the orders of the devil.

On the south slope of Pratt Hill in Upton, where the famous megalithic chamber sits, the devil's footprints are spread two miles apart. Both footprints are five feet long and two feet wide, facing southward.

This one is by far one of my favorite tales of New Enlgand. The story of Jonathon Moulton and how he tried to trick the devil is a classic example of our Yankee ingenuity and shrewd business sense. Moulton was born in Hampton, New Hampshire, on July 22, 1726. In his youth, he was an apprentice to a cabinetmaker but was able to buy his freedom in 1745 at age nineteen. In that year, he married Abigail Smith, and the couple had eleven children. Moulton would go on to serve as a captain in the French and Indian War and later became a general. He also served as a representative for the New Hampshire legislature. He became quite the businessman, having once said that he could get the best of anybody, including the devil. One night, Moulton was sitting by the fire contemplating how he could further enrich his already wealthy estate. It was then that he proclaimed to no one in particular that he would gladly sell his soul to the devil for riches beyond his imagination.

Suddenly there was a stir from the chimney, and black soot fell over the hearth. Out popped a slender man in a black velvet cape and hat. Jonathon Moulton was taken aback for a spell but regained his composure and realized

Pine Grove Cemetery in Hampton, New Hampshire, is where Jonathon Moulton's memorial marker sits.

that he was face to face with the Prince of Darkness. "Why, you are the…," Moulton began.

"What do names matter. Do you want to make a bargain or not?" said the devil as he picked up a glowing coal and held it up to his watch. "I have an appointment of the same in Portsmouth in less than a quarter hour's time so let's be quick, shall we?"

The general was astounded at the figure's sentence, as Portsmouth was at least five leagues from his home in Hampton, yet the word "bargain" was all Moulton needed to hear. The devil then reached into his pocket and let loose a pile of gold coins to the floor. The general swiftly snatched at one of the coins but quickly threw it aside as it burned his hand. The devil gave out a haughty guffaw at his action. "Go ahead; pick it up." The devil said.

"But it is as hot as a blacksmith's fire."

"Trust me and pick up the coin." When Moulton touched the coin a second time, it was cool. He bit it, banged it on the table and even weighed the piece. Sure enough, it was pure gold.

The devil then asked for something to drink. Moulton produced two glasses and a flask of rum. The devil gallantly emptied his glass with a smack of his lips and continued. "There is plenty more where that came from. All you need to do is sign this contract and once a month, hang a pair of boots from the crane in the fireplace, and they will be filled with gold come morning. All I ask for in return is your soul. But I warn you, Jonathon Moulton, do not try to fool the devil, or you will suffer dire consequence. I know of your dealings and will be carefully watching you."

The devil then unrolled a parchment and took a pen from his belt, dipped it in ink and handed it to his new friend. Moulton became overwhelmed with the possible arrangement and hesitated for a spell. "Come on, General. We have not got all day. Either it is a deal or not." Jonathon Moulton then took his glass filled with rum and quaffed it quickly. As he went to sign the paper, he noticed the names of several other prominent citizens who had inked their signatures before him. "At least I will be in good company," he mumbled to himself.

This being done, General Moulton scoured the countryside in search of the largest pair of boots he could find and hung them faithfully as the devil requested. Each time, once a month, they would be filled with gold coins. It was not long before Jonathon Moulton figured that he would up the stakes a bit. He was wealthy beyond his wildest dreams, but he could not resist his own knack for getting the better of his end of a bargain.

When the devil went to fill his boots on the Ides of March in 1769, he found that no matter how much he put in, the leathers would not load up. Satan pulled one of the boots from the hearth and found that not only was the sole cut out, they were also placed over holes cut in the floor so the gold streamed into the cellar. The irate devil immediately flew into a hellish rage and burned the house to the ground. Moulton searched and searched for the gold he had hidden within the rafters and foundation of the home, but not a single ounce of the precious ore was to be found. General Moulton died in 1787. His first wife had passed in 1775, and he remarried shortly after. Both he and his first wife were buried on the property, but their graves have long since disappeared. Perhaps he had to fulfill his side of the bargain after all. It is rumored that the first Mrs. Moulton haunted the home that the general rebuilt after his pact with the devil.

The devil has also left his calling card in Ipswich, Massachusetts. According to George Nutting in his book *Massachusetts: A Guide to Its Places and People*, "On the North Green stood the First Parish Church, built in 1635. Deep in the rock beside the present Congregational building (1847) is a cloven hoof print left, legend says, by the Devil."

As the legends states, Satan tried to conceal himself within the church, where he could create havoc. For this act, he was hurled from the steeple

Jonathon Moulton's stone in Pine Grove Cemetery in Hampton is only a memorial. General Moulton is not buried here, as his exact whereabouts remain a mystery to this day.

top by some unseen instrument of righteousness with such force that his hoof mark was stamped into the boulder below. This did not deter him from mounting the ridgepole and assuming a defiant air with folded arms when the preacher Whitefield began his holy sermon. The preacher's tremendous voice was enough to shake the pole and send the devil once again into the air in terror, and with that, the evil one flew off and disappeared.

The town of Portsmouth, New Hampshire, once had a run-in with the dark one, but the story takes on the tone of revenge rather than the malicious mischief for which the devil is perennially known. In 1682, there lived a widow in a small abode on a petite but attractive parcel of land. Her neighbor, George Walton, wished to obtain her real estate, finding it most desirable for his needs. The old woman had no family or friends to account for, so Walton accused her of witchcraft and in due time somehow gained possession of her property. The charge of witchcraft was dropped, but the poor woman was cast out in the cold with no home left to return to.

Having been swindled out of her land, the old woman laid a curse on the place, asserting that he would never have a day's rest or know any pleasure from his gain. The man scoffed at her curse and sent her away. Then he moved his family into the old woman's house. The Sunday preceding her ouster from her former property, the family had gone to bed thinking nothing of the curse. At ten o'clock, the inhabitants of the household were stirred from their sleep by a bombardment of stones against the roof and doors of the home. At first, they thought that Indians were mounting an assault on the home, but when they peered cautiously through the windows, they saw the moonlit fields void of movement. All at once, the gate lifted from its post and flew through the air, disappearing into the darkness. As Charles Skinner put it in his book *Myths and Legends of Our Land*, "Walton ventured out, but a volley of stones, seemingly from a hundred hands, was delivered at his head, and he ran back to shelter. Doors and windows were barred and shuttered, but it made no difference. Stones, too hot to hold a hand upon, were hurled through glass and down the chimney."

The "stone throwing devil" was not limited to just hurling rocks. Objects in the rooms began to take wing and fly at Walton when he passed by. Candles would extinguish themselves, cheese spoiled, haystacks in the fields became dispersed all over the ground and thrown in trees, there was tapping at the window and even the locks and keys were found bent and damaged beyond repair.

While Walton paced the floor, a sledgehammer flew overhead, landing with a loud *thud* just in front of him. Upon impact, the hammer put a dent in the heavy oak floor. An iron was driven into a wall and a kettle hung upon it. A guest staying with the family began to play a musical instrument when a stone rolled into the room, coming to rest in front of him. There was also pounding from various rooms that would resonate throughout the home, shaking it to its very foundation. These were just a few of the malicious tricks that plagued the Walton family. For the longest time, Walton could not venture past the threshold of his home without being assailed by a volley of stones aimed directly at him.

Even Peter Stuyvesant encountered the devil one moonlit night while trying to row through Hell Gate. The devil saw him approaching and made an attempt to accost the famous settler. As Stuyvesant rowed closer, Satan noticed what he thought was Struyvesant's wooden leg on his shoulder. Before he could react, the devil realized that it was a gun loaded with a silver bullet, blessed with prayer. The bullet passed through the devil's ribs, and the dark one exploded with an unearthly scream as an overwhelming reek of sulfur burned the man's nostrils. The bullet landed on Ward's Island, where three boys later picked it up and traded it for a healthy sum of doughnuts.

In case you are wondering where the devil bides his time when not wreaking havoc on the people of New England, there are plenty of "devil's dens" in the region where the horned one can rest his weary tail. Some include but are not limited to devil's dens in Auburn, New Hampshire; Andover, North Berwick and Porter, Maine; Mount Tabor in Rutland County, Vermont; Bradford, Vermont; Sterling Connecticut; Weston, Connecticut; Newbury, Massachusetts; Ashland, Massachusetts; Smithfield, Rhode Island; and even a Devil's Den Bed-and-Breakfast in Chelsea, Vermont.

What Does Webster Lake's Real Name Mean?

You can always tell a native of Webster, Massachusetts. All you need do is ask them about their hometown lake, and the name flows from their lips like a verse of elegant poetry. "You must mean Lake Chargoggagoggmanchauggagoggchaubunagungamaugg," they will say so fluidly. Affectionately known as Webster Lake, this body of water made up of three ponds and two "narrows" is the pride of the town, as much of the revenues go toward the upkeep and preservation of the lake. In the summer months, the beach is a popular destination for families to wile away the day in the hot sun while cooling off in the crisp, clean water. The lake has an illustrious history, as related from the Indians of the region.

Originally, the Town of Oxford purchased the land and lake from the Nipmuc tribe in 1681. It became a permanent settlement in 1713. In 1811, Samuel Slater built a spinning mill above North Pond near the little village of Manchaug.

What does the name actually translate to in English? Well, the popular answer told by most is that the saying means, "You fish on your side, I fish on my side and nobody fishes in the middle." Legend says that two Indian tribes lived on both sides of the lake—one on the North Pond shore and the other at South Pond. They both felt that they had the inalienable right to fish Middle Pond, and a long debate ensued over who could fish the middle. Finally, they came to an agreement that they would fish in their respective ponds and no one would fish in Middle Pond. Lawrence Daly of the *Webster Times* is credited with the origin of this legend, and his comical translation that has stuck to this day. The only problem is that it is not true. Daly admitted plenty of times that it was just a story made for fun, but somehow the people embraced the meaning with gusto.

The principal tribe was the Nipmucs, whose name basically means "freshwater fishermen." The lake, with its surrounding majestic scenery and many islands, provided plenty of fish and game for the Indians. It was also believed that the Great Spirit resided in the lake, and those who went on after death joined him to forever hunt and fish in this happy hunting ground. They also believed that the islands were inhabited by benevolent spirits. John Eliot and Daniel Gookin established a praying village there in 1674, creating a sacred meeting place for those to come and worship. Beacon Park is presently on the site of that former village. How the lake ended up with its present name is a bit convoluted, but there are historical timelines that help to clear the matter somewhat.

In 1642, Nathaniel Woodward and Solomon Saffery, while surveying the colonial boundaries in New England, discovered the lake. They named it Great Pond. John Winthrop later called it Lake Squabage, but a treaty between John Eliot and the local Indians in 1668 is where we first see the name in much shorter form. In the treaty, the words Monuhchogok and Chaubunakongkomuk are mentioned—the former representing the name of the Indians in the area that would later become Manchaugagogg and the latter meaning "a boundary place" or "fishing place at the boundary."

By 1717, the name had become Chaubunagungamoag, with a few variances of the spelling as time went by. But in the Dudley town plan of 1795, the lake is named Chargoggagoggmanchoggaggogg. A map of 1795 showing the town of Dudley indicated the lake's name as Chargoggaggoggmanchoggagogg. In 1831, both Dudley and Oxford, which adjoined the lake, filed maps listing the name of the pond as Chargoggagoggmanchoggagogg. What does this translate to, you ask? "Chargoggagogg" is said to translate into "knifemen" or "Englishmen" who carry swords. So, basically, we have so far something in the way of "Englishmen who carry swords (or "English knifemen") and Nipmuc Indians." This would make sense as early settlers were always armed and ready for anything this strange New World could throw at them. It would also make sense regarding the treaty by Eliot making the place a neutral fishing and hunting zone. Another translation comes forth, however, making Chargoggagoggmanchauggagogg "Englishmen at Manchaug."

As time went on, the name was lengthened and then shortened and then lengthened again until it reached its present forty-five-letter moniker. The exact translation is a matter of ever-growing controversy, but what can best be thought by one camp is, "English knifemen and Nipmuc Indians at the Boundary or Neutral Fishing Place."

There is the other claim that the name derives from the time Samuel Slater built his mills near the lake close to Manchaug Village. Chargoggagoggmanchauggagoggchaubunagungamaugg would then translate to "English at Manchaug at the Fishing Place at the Boundary." This makes sense, given that the word "Manchaug" is built into the name.

Whatever its exact meaning may be, it is still the longest place name in the United States and the third-longest in the English language. Perhaps it is easier to remember it as the "You fish on your side, I fish on my side and nobody fishes in the middle" Lake.

RAMTAIL

The Untold Story

Decades ago, I embarked on a journey. This expedition was not one logged by miles but by time and space. Although the destination is but a few towns away, hundreds of years have passed and yet the search grows longer with every stone unturned. I have written much on the legend of the Ramtail Factory in Foster, Rhode Island, but as time has given me more facts and history, I feel I must share with my readers all that has been uncovered and then some that may still lie in the dark bowers of history.

On March 20, 1813, five partners—William Potter; his son, Olney; William's brother-in-law, Jonathon Ellis; and his sons-in-law Marvin Round and Peleg Walker—purchased six acres of land from Parley Round along the Ponaganset River and began the largest attempt at a water-powered factory in Foster history. On June 29, 1814, another parcel of land adjacent to the first lot was purchased for the expansion of the project. The factory, the Foster Woolen Manufactory, comprised a mill, a waste house, a blacksmith shop, five millhouses and a company store. Some claim that there may have been a boardinghouse, but there is no definitive record of one. The reason it was called "Ramtail" is somewhat speculative. One account states that someone once brought in ram tails to be made into cloth. Another reason comes from the small pieces of wool that would rise from the cloth, as it was being prepared or "napped." When these whisks were sheared to make the cloth even, they would fall to the floor in little curls resembling a ram's tail.

Legend tells us that Peleg Walker was designated as night watchman for the establishment. When night fell on the tiny mill hamlet, it was Peleg's duty,

The stone foundation is all that remains of the Ramtail Factory in Foster.

with lantern in hand, to make his rounds securing the factory and watching over the investments until the break of dawn, where he would end his shift by ringing the mill bell, thus summoning the workers to their daily toils. The little homes were decorated with small gardens and day lilies, making them a picturesque scene of tranquility and harmony within the tiny village. If one ventures into the remains of the village, one of the first vestiges that stands to greet the traveler are the day lilies that still grow abundantly amid the trees, brush and scrub oak.

At one point, there was an argument over money, and Peleg was said to have warned the rest of the partners that one day they would have to take the keys to the mill from a dead man's pocket. On the morning of May 19, 1822, the mill bell failed to ring, and the perplexed villagers gathered at the mill but could not gain entry. Senior partner William Potter finally arrived and broke a window to gain access. When they entered the mill, a ghastly sight awaited them. There hanging from the bell rope was thirty-five-year-old Peleg Walker, keys to the mill dangling from his pocket.

A few days later, he was buried in the Potter plot overlooking Hopkins Mill Pond. The villagers could resume their normal routine, or so they thought. One night, shortly after the funeral, the bell began to peal at the exact hour of midnight. When Olney Potter and a few of the braver neighbors entered the mill, the ringing mysteriously ceased. This event transpired several more times before the Potters removed the bell rope. This did not stop Peleg, for the bell continued to toll at midnight, leaving the owners with no choice but to completely remove the bell.

One night, the villagers were roused from their slumber by the sound of the mill running full tilt. One of the workers was able to gain entry and shut it down, but the next night, the same event occurred. This time the crowd stood in horror as it beheld the wheel turning opposite the flow of the river.

At this point, no one would work at the haunted factory, and people began to leave the little village. Peleg's spirit was spotted once shortly after. A few locals passing by the factory one night saw his ghost. They noticed a glowing specter, lantern in hand, moving about the factory buildings. They immediately recognized the gait as that of Peleg Walker.

In 1873, the factory burned to its foundation, but this did not stop Peleg from making his rounds. Even today, locals hear the ominous phantom bell tolling at the witching hour and have seen the glow of a candle lantern drifting through the air, held by some unseen hands. The haunting has had such an impact on the region that it is listed in the 1885 state census on page 36, where it simply states, "Ram Tail Factory, (haunted)."

That is the usual story one will hear when inquiring about the Ramtail haunt, but there is much more to the story than legend would divulge. Many of us have a favorite haunt or story that seems to become our passion, and the story of the Ramtail factory captured my interest immediately upon my first read. Being spellbound with the legend of Ramtail, I endeavored to find out everything I could about its history, its people and, of course, its ghosts.

Starting with town records, a fire did actually destroy many personal records from 1785 to 1810. The records were kept in Scituate, the town bordering Foster at the time, and a fire in the clerk's office obliterated much of what we could have used to learn about Peleg Walker and his early life. Whatever records exist pertaining to Ramtail are well preserved and in good order at the Foster Town Hall. Between the two town's records and countless trips to the site, I made some remarkable discoveries that seem to change the legend as we know it.

First of all, Peleg was not a night watchman. His manner of dress and status as esquire would relate that he was what he proclaimed to be in his deeds, a manufacturer. He purchased several lots of land and at one point owed the factory a substantial sum of money. His probate records show that he owned fine furniture, a horse shay (a light two-wheel carriage) and an extensive wardrobe and that he owned stock in the turnpike and school.

Looking across the Ponaganset River, one can easily see the dam and bridge abutment at the haunted Ramtail Factory site.

In 1822, before he died, he began to sell much of his holdings. It appears that he spent more than he earned, and the partners wanted their money. Being family, it can be assumed that a deal may have been made whereby he was ousted from the partnership and relegated to something of a night watchman. A few strange deeds found in the town hall seem to have a suspicious nature about them. As stated before, Peleg died on May 19, 1822. It has been generally accepted that if one committed suicide in those days, there would be no record of their deaths due to the shame on the family, but to the contrary, the Arnold Vital Records of Rhode Island states on page 207, under Walker, "Peleg, Esq., at Foster, suddenly May 19, 1822."

The presence of a record showed me that maybe his death was not a suicide. Perhaps there was more to it, but that is just speculation. Then there are the two deeds drawn up the night before his death. The first deed is made out to William Potter, senior partner and patriarch of the family and factory, the second to William's son, Olney. The first deed, dated May 17, 1822, gives William Potter a quarter of Peleg's shares and rights in the factory and the twenty-five acres of land that Peleg's father, William Walker, gave him in 1810, presumably when he married William Potter's daughter, Mary.

The second deed relays his last quarter-share of the factory and all its equipment and tools to Olney Potter. Both deeds are written in completely different handwriting, and Peleg's name is signed and sealed by the scriber of each separate deed. One of the strangest details pertaining to these deeds is that they were drawn up at quarter to one o'clock in the morning—what a strange time to do business in 1822. Most people went to bed with the setting of the sun and rose at the first break of dawn. What created the need to draw these deeds up at such an unusual time? Kerosene lamps would not exist until 1853, when they were first introduced in Germany. This means that the work would have been done by the dim glow of candlelight. Why would they be in such a hurry to transfer these possessions? Mary, who always cosigned all deeds with Peleg, did not sign either of the deeds in question but did add an addendum on July 4, 1822, approving the transaction with her brother, Olney. Also, in June of that year, William Potter quitclaimed the twenty-five acres of land from his midnight deed back to William Walker. This was the piece of their land that William Walker gave his son, Peleg, in 1810.

One other fact that really stands out is the legend that Peleg hanged himself from the bell rope. There are several writings that state that he slit his throat, including one from a family diary of a woman, Mrs. Williams, who worked at the mill during that time and witnessed the blood everywhere. Another important fact that cannot be overlooked is that May 19, 1822, fell on a Sunday. No one worked on Sundays during that time, so why would they be waiting for a bell to ring? How would they know to break into the factory (if in truth they actually did) to find Mr. Walker? Being very religious in those days, Sunday was truly a day of rest and worship. In many cases, whole villages and towns were disincorporated for lack of a proper meetinghouse. Who knows what really happened on May 19, 1822?

The truth is that we still have a haunted site, a famous legend and a lot of mystery. Legend has a way of taking strange turns off the beaten path of fact. It may seem more romantic to have an argument, a foreboding threat and then a suicide that make the story ripe for a haunt. Perhaps there was an argument, but it did not go as the legend tells us. Some people think that Peleg may have met an untimely demise at the hand of one of the partners. That would make for a whole other legend in and of itself. The inscription on Peleg's stone reads, "Life how short. Eternity how long." This is not an uncommon inscription, but it does tend to add to the legend when all things are considered. You have an argument, a suicide and a ghost bound to make his eternal rounds of the factory that he so much loved in life. Mix in the epitaph, and the story gets even more alluring. An interesting thing to note

Peleg Walker's weather-beaten stone in the Potter burial ground overlooking Hopkins Mill Pond. The worn inscription ("Life how short. Eternity how long.") was a fairly common epitaph for the times.

is that Olney Potter—although his stone states May 15, 1831, as his death date—is listed in the Arnold records as having died on May 19, 1831. If the date of his death was May 19, we have an exact calendar date of nine years. If the date of Olney's death was the one carved into his stone, he died on the third Sunday in May, just as Peleg did. On both days, the sun rose at 4:40 a.m. and set at 7:20 p.m. Truly, this would be exactly nine years to the day from Peleg's death. Perhaps it's the power of threes, I've been told.

Rebecca Cornell's
"Unhappie Accident of Fire"

D o you believe that the spirit of someone can actually come back and provide evidence of their demise? In 1673, there were those who became convinced that a ghost actually attested to her own murder. In the court records of Portsmouth, Rhode Island, evidence of such a supernatural act is penned in spidery handwriting for all to peruse.

Thomas Cornell, born in about 1593 in Essex, England, married Rebecca Briggs (born in 1600) and came to the New World in about 1636, settling in Boston, where he was permitted (by town meeting) to purchase the former property of William Baulstone. He was also granted a permit for an inn. In 1637, Ann Hutchinson and her fellow Antinomians were expelled from Boston. This included Thomas and his family, along with his brother-in-law, John Briggs. They then purchased land from Canonicus and Miantonomi that would later become Newport. They settled on the north of the island, calling it Portsmouth.

Thomas actually arrived two years later, on August 6, 1640. In February 1641, he was granted a piece of land and became constable. The spelling "Cornhill" (or "Cornill") also appears in the old records. Thomas died in 1655. A will reportedly drawn up December 5, 1651, left to his wife, Rebecca, all of his real estate upon his death. Rebecca had a will, dated September 2, 1664, that left her son, Thomas, all of her land lying on the west side of Rhode Island between the farms of Thomas Hazard and John Coggeshall. Neither will is known to exist as of this writing. Entries in the records kept by the Society of Friends at Portsmouth are all we have to piece together this portion of the life and circumstance of the Cornell family.

Around 1657, Rebecca began to both will and divvy out holdings that her husband had accrued during his travels in the New World. Ten acres that were granted to her husband were deeded to her son and daughter. In 1661, she sold two parcels of land containing eight acres, a house and fruit trees to Richard Hart. Her son Thomas confirmed this. Thomas witnessed much of his inheritance dwindle away to pay for daily expenses accrued after his father's death. On October 25, 1663, Rebecca conveyed one-sixth of a share of land now in Dartmouth to her son Joshua. On July 27 of that year, she deeded to Thomas all her housing, orchard and fencing in Portsmouth. She held a one-hundred-pound bond of Thomas's at her death. She conveyed other portions of property in Dartmouth to her other sons. This may sound trivial at present, but as you read on, you may begin to wonder what really happened and why.

A curious entry from the Friends Records dated February 8, 1673, notes, "Rebecca Cornell, widow, was killed strangely at Portsmouth in her own dwelling house, was twice viewed by the Coroner's Inquest and buried again by her husband's grave in their own land."

The *Arnold Vital Records of Rhode Island, 1636–1850*, volume 7 (*Friends and Ministers*), states, "Cornell, Rebecca, widow, Portsmouth, killed strangely at her house, 8 Feb, 1672." These entries tell nothing of the story of what transpired after the death of Rebecca Cornell. They are a preamble to what has become one of the most bizarre legends of New England. But what about her death itself? Lets start with that.

On February 8, 1673, Rebecca Cornell was discovered burned to death in her room. The original coroner's inquest given on February 9, the next day, labeled it as an "unhappie accident of fire," but that would change rather quickly. It appeared that Mrs. Cornell had nestled down in her chair by the fire with a pipe in hand. Either an ember from the fire or a coal from the pipe somehow ignited her top and quickly spread, consuming her in flames. When found, she was barely recognizable. Within days of being laid to rest, her brother, John Briggs, was roused from his sleep by a bright light at the foot of his bed. He immediately recognized it as the glowing visage of Rebecca. She then faded away. Briggs then went to the coroner's inquest, and a second examination showed that there might have been foul play. Briggs was convinced that she was intentionally set on fire. The suspicion fell on her son Thomas, who had been in the room with her for roughly one and a half hours on the night she died and was the last to see her alive.

An investigation was held, and Thomas was arrested for the murder of his mother. Testimony revealed much about that evening.

The neglected Cornell lot in the woods of Portsmouth, Rhode Island. Rebecca is buried there, but it is unclear if Thomas was as well since many of the stones are unmarked or missing.

John Briggs (or Brigs), born in Darrington, England, in 1609, married Thomas Cornell Sr.'s sister, Sarah, with whom they had six children. Sarah died in 1667. Briggs held several important positions in the colonies. His influence would no doubt be instrumental in the trial that would follow. On February 20, 1673, Briggs testified that on the twelfth of February, four days after Rebecca had died, he laid in bed and

> *being betweene sleepeing and wakeing, as he thought he felt something heave up the Bedclothes twice, and thought somebody had beene coming to bed to hime, where upon he Awaked, and turned himeselfe about in his bed, and being turned, he perceived a light in the roome like to the dawning of ye day, and plainely saw the shape and appearance of a woman standing by his bedside where at he was much affrighted, and cryed out, in the name of God, what art thou, the Aperition answered, I am your sister Cornell, and twice sayd, see how I was Burnt with ffire, and she plainely apeered unto him to be very much burnt about the shoulders, fface and head.*

This vision was perceived by Briggs to be a sign that his sister had met with foul play, prompting a second coroner's inquest. Mrs. Cornell was disinterred and examined once more. This time, they found a suspicious wound on the uppermost part of her stomach. This along with the fire was concluded as attributing to her death.

Among those examined were Thomas Cornell Jr.; his wife, Sarah; Henry Straite; John Russill; George Soule; James Moills; John Cornell, who was the son of Thomas and Sarah; and John's wife, Mary.

Apparently, Straite was a lodger at the Cornell home when the incident occurred. When he asked why Mrs. Cornell was not at supper, Thomas told him that she did not like salted mackerel, as it makes her dry at night. After dinner, Sarah sent one of the boys to see if his grandmother might want boiled milk for supper. The boy returned seeking a candle to see what the fire was in the room. The dinner party rushed to the room, and Straite, being the first to enter, saw a fire on the floor and raked it away with his hands. He then noticed the figure on the floor and, thinking it may have been a drunken Indian, began to speak in their language toward the figure. Thomas then cried out, "Oh Lord, it is my mother."

Straite, along with the others, noticed that the bed curtains and valance were burned but had been put out. He also stated that other times when they had mackerel for supper, Mrs. Cornell would dine with them. James Moills, upon examination, said pretty much the same thing.

Thomas Cornell, son of Thomas and Sarah, testified that he and his father were in the room with Mrs. Cornell the night she died. He left, and his father stayed in the room for about one hour more before coming out to supper, stating that Mrs. Cornell would not be joining them that evening.

Others testified that Thomas and Sarah treated the old woman very badly, neglecting her needs and never offering any aid to her. Mary Cornell stated that when she once visited the home, Mrs. Cornell was forced to chase after the pigs herself, as her son offered no help, and noted that she was weak and tired. She mentioned that she desired to stab a penknife into her heart to end her troubles but chose to "resist ye devil" instead. There was also testimony that she had mentioned being denied food and blankets or a warm fire in the cold of winter. George Soule testified that Mrs. Cornell had told him that she was going to go live with her son Samuel come spring if she was not first disposed of or made away. She also told Soule that there had been a conflict with Thomas about the rent and one-hundred-pound bond that Thomas wanted her to forget if he was going to further pay any rent to her.

Thomas also had a chance to declare his version of what happened that evening. His testimony followed along with the others, having spent some time alone with his mother before coming out to supper with the rest of the

The Cornell Home in Portsmouth is presently the Valley Inn. The original home burned down in 1899 and was reconstructed to the same specifications.

party present. He also saw the figure on the floor upon entering the room. While Mr. Straite spoke in Indian to the figure, he noticed by candlelight that the shoes were his mother's. He cried out, "Oh Lord, it is my mother" and took her head in his arms to see if she was still alive. He also noted that the bed curtains and valance had been burned but had since been extinguished.

It was also noted that the wool she wore was burned, while the cotton was not. It should have been the exact opposite, as women of the times wore wool while working around fire, as wool does not burn but rather only smolders. This way, the wearer would be safe from having their clothes ignite while cooking or tending to the fireplace.

Based on these testimonies and mostly on the vision of John Briggs, Thomas Cornell was found guilty of murdering his mother and was sentenced to hang at about one o'clock on May 23, 1673. Cornell did not appeal the sentence but asked permission to be buried next to his mother. The judge denied his request but granted him the permission to be buried in an unmarked grave within twenty feet of the common road. Whether that road is Route 114 or a once common lane near the cemetery is a matter of conjecture. The aforementioned road could be the present West Main Road.

Above: The old Colony House in Newport sits where the original wooden one was before it was torn down to make way for the more elaborate brick structure. The Newport Common, where Thomas Cornell was executed, still graces the front of the building.

Left: One of the many old "hangman" trees in Newport. Whether the tree Thomas Cornell was hanged from still stands today is unknown.

If this is correct, Thomas is buried somewhere under the driveway of his former home, now the Valley Inn.

This did not end the saga of Rebecca Cornell. Roughly one year later, an Indian named Wickhapasg, known to the locals as Harry, was tried as an accomplice for the murder but acquitted. Thomas's brother William also pointed the finger at Sarah, accusing her of having an involvement in his mother's demise. She, too, was acquitted.

This is a rather strange case. The vision of a ghost sent her son to the gallows. The court records, available for all to see, tell the story. Of course, upon reading the testimonies, scholars, present-day lawyers and scores of others do not believe that Thomas was guilty of murdering his mother. In fact, his wife, pregnant at the time of his execution, named their daughter Innocent Cornell in protest of the unjust treatment of her husband. Innocent Cornell, born in 1673, married Richard Borden in 1691. She was the great-great-great-great-grandmother of Lizzie Borden of Fall River, Massachusetts, who was arrested and tried for the August 4, 1892 murders of her father, Andrew, and her stepmother, Abbie Borden. Lizzie, unlike her ancestor, was acquitted in the murders and died in 1927 at the age of sixty-six. To this day, the Borden case remains as one of the most famous unsolved murders in New England (if not American) history. The Borden family is buried at Oak Hill Cemetery in Fall River.

THE UNFORTUNATE HANNAH ROBINSON

Ｎew England is a treasure-trove of remarkable legends, places and people. This next story has been handed down through the centuries, but like most narratives, the accounts have managed to take on many different guises suited to fit the mood of the teller. Digging through family histories can sometimes turn up conflicting details in the story of one's life, depending on the person relating that tale and how partial the narrator was to the people being immortalized in prose.

Rowland Robinson, born in 1719 as the oldest son of Governor William Robinson, was named after his grandfather, who was a wealthy farmer active in the political body of the colonies. Robinson was portly, tall and erect, with a clear blonde complexion and light hair. He was known to be fair in temper and manners, having the disposition of an old country gentleman. It is accounted in *Recollections of Olden Times* by Thomas Hazard that Mr. Robinson, with others of his day, sent a ship to the Guinea coast in order to procure slaves for work on his farm. He was to select the finest of the lot and sell the portion he saw unfit for his needs. Up until the arrival of this ship, Mr. Robinson had no idea of the cruelty and injustice that these people endured:

> *But now when he saw the forlorn, woe-begone looking men and women who had been huddled together like beasts, disembarking, some of them too feeble to stand alone, the enormity of his offense against humanity presented itself so vividly to his susceptible mind that he wept like a child, nor would he consent that a single slave which fell to his share—twenty-eight in all—*

should be sold, but took them all to his own home where, though held in servitude, were kindly cared for.

One woman, named Abigail, took a special liking to the New World and asked her boss if it would be too much for her only son to be brought from her homeland to join her at the farm. This he granted at his own expense.

On December 3, 1741, Rowland married Anstis Gardiner, daughter of John Gardiner, at St. Paul's Church in Narragansett. Dr. Reverend McSparran presided over the ceremony. They had three children: Hannah, born in 1746; Mary, born in 1752; and William R., born in 1759. Mary and Hannah grew to be exceedingly beautiful, especially Hannah, who stood above medium height and had a clear complexion, with a delicate tint of rose that only served to complement her dark hazel eyes. Her auburn hair fell in ringlets about her frame, and her speech, manner and carriage made her all the more irresistible to the gentry both near and far.

In her youth, Hannah found a place where she could sit and contemplate or just enjoy the scenery of the Narragansett Bay. The area, known as McSparran Hill, was steep and bore forth a rock ledge that admitted a clear view of the bay. Hannah wiled away many hours looking out over the beautiful scenery the ledge afforded her.

The Robinson family spared no cost in the education of their children. Hannah was placed in the care of her aunt in Newport, where she attended the finishing school of Madame Osborne, a well-respected and widely known instructor of politeness and grace for young ladies. It was during her studies with Madame Osborne that Hannah met M. Pierre Simons (later known as Peter), a young tutor under the employ of Osborne. Simons was of a notable Huguenot family who had fled France, arriving in Newport during the Protestant persecutions under the reign of Louis XIV. From the moment they met, a certain affection ripened between them that would soon turn into pure, undaunted love.

Both were well aware that a person of his station in life would certainly not meet the expectations of her father as a proper suitor. Two books—*Recollections of Olden Times*, by Thomas Robinson Hazard and Willis Pope Hazard from 1879, and *The Robinsons and Their Kin Folk*, by the Robinson Family Genealogical Association, written in 1906—tell the tale with very little variance. The 1906 version reads:

Fortune seemed to favor the young people: Hannah's uncle, Col. William Gardiner, educated his children at home, and in looking about for a private tutor, engaged Pierre Simons to go with him to his Narragansett home and occupy that position in his family. The lovers enjoyed many opportunities of seeing each other, especially as Col. Gardiner, who was of a kind and easy disposition, on becoming aware of the love which existed between his beautiful niece and her former tutor, sought rather to promote opportunities for interviews between the lovers than otherwise.

The mother's suspicions were aroused, and Hannah confided to her the secret of her love.

After trying for months, in vain, to persuade her child to discourage her affianced lover, and finding that nothing would induce her to dismiss him, Mrs. Robinson forbore further opposition.

Thus encouraged by the mother's tacit consent, if not approval of his suit, it was mutually arranged by the lovers that Pierre should occasionally walk over from Col. Gardiner's of an evening, and upon the appearance of a signal light in Hannah's window approach the house and secrete himself in a large lilac bush which grew beneath it, where love messages might be easily passed. In fact, so emboldened did the lovers become by the unbroken success that attended their stratagem, that they finally arranged for occasional meetings in Hannah's room; her mother lending her presence and countenance to the dangerous adventure, rendered all the more critical because of its being the undeviating practice of Hannah's father to bid her "good night" before he retired, even if it required his going to her own room or elsewhere. It was necessary to have a convenient place in which Hannah's lover might retreat on untoward occasions Such a place—a cupboard—was in the room.

In 1889, J.R. Cole mentioned the same cupboard as still being a part of the room. It would suffice to say that Hannah, although just entering adulthood, had already gathered a fair number of suitors, some from the finest families in the region. Yet all of these fine, educated and wealthy prospects were of no interest to the young beauty.

One evening, Rowland happened to step outside the home and saw Hannah reaching out her window to the young Simons. He recognized the man right away as the music teacher employed by his brother-in-law, William Gardiner. The very thought of his lovely daughter throwing herself at a lowly dance instructor enraged the otherwise temperate man. He gave chase to Simons, flailing his cane at him, but was unable to catch the fleet-footed young wooer. From that moment on, Hannah's every move was watched—if she walked, she walked with spying eyes. When she rode, a servant accompanied her. Her father became obsessive in keeping her under his watch at every waking moment. Such conditions began to take a toll on her health and wholesome appearance. It became the whisper around town that many would like to see the young woman be with her love and began to prepare for an elopement, especially her mother and aunt, Mrs. Ludowick Updike, sister of Rowland.

A great ball was planned at the Updike home, now known as Smith's Castle. It was arranged that the two sisters, Mary and Hannah, would attend the ball and stay overnight with the Updikes. Rowland had no objection to this idea, as he assumed that she would be watched well by the family. He had no idea that his family would bring his daughter into the arms of the rogue he most despised. Hannah went about her way in a composed manner until it was time to leave for the ball. Then, with her watchers in tow, they mounted their horses and rode off toward the soiree. *The Robinsons and Their Kin Folk* notes:

> *On Ridge Hill, a thickly wooded spot, Hannah and her companions encountered the lover with a closed carriage, into which the affianced bride hastily stepped and was driven rapidly away, on the road to Providence, in spite of the frantic appeals of Prince, the attendant. Miss Simons—Pierre's sister—assisted Hannah with a necessary wardrobe, and with the aid of the pastoral services of a minister of the Episcopal Church, the lovers were married.*

When Mr. Robinson learned of his daughter's elopement, he became angry beyond comprehension. He went as far as offering a reward to anyone who would come forth with any information or names of those who assisted in her escapade. Much to his disappointment, no one ever came forth.

Simons and his bride resided with his father until he found employment in Providence. I find two complete versions of the story from here. As time passed, Simons began to realize that Hannah would never see a penny of her family's fortune. This caused him to become unreceptive to his wife's affection toward him. He began to have affairs, became reckless in his habit and eventually turned a complete cold shoulder to her.

Hannah, already unstable in spirit, took a turn for the worst. She became gaunt and pale, a shadow of her former beauty. Her mother, who stayed in distant contact, arranged for Hannah to be reunited with her dog, Marcus, and servant, also named Hannah. Both joined the young woman in Providence, which gave Hannah some solace, but her broken heart would not heal. Her father, upon hearing of her rapid decline in health, rode to Providence in the hopes of bringing her home, but under his terms. Mr. Robinson rode out to her home and, without dismounting, rapped on the door with his cane. Hannah's servant answered, and Rowland gave his pitch: if Hannah would tell him who was responsible for her elopement, she could come back to the warmth and care of her family home. Hannah was honorable but also possessed the same stubborn streak as her father. When the servant returned to the door saying that Hannah had refused his wishes, Mr. Robinson rode away in a huff, but he would return almost every day and inquire of her condition.

Then came the day that Mr. Robinson finally agreed to let Hannah come home. He summoned up his strength and decided to see Hannah in person. When he entered her chamber, he was not ready for the sight he beheld. There was his daughter, frail and white, almost every ounce of life dissipated from her body. He began to cry like a baby and completely dismissed the thought of asking Hannah to divulge the accomplices of that fateful evening. Instead, he held her cold, bony hand and promised to take her home. He then gave the servant some gold pieces to prepare for departure back to the Robinson Homestead. Mr. Robinson had Hannah placed in a litter for safe travel back to Narragansett. (A litter is a carriage with no wheels that usually has two long poles running lengthwise supporting it; the poles can be grasped and carried by hand. Litters became rare in the nineteenth century as the roads improved.)

The carriers, called "chairmen," lifted the litter with Hannah and set out for home. When they reached Old Ridge Hill, where Hannah had met with her lover that fateful night, she covered her eyes and cried. As they passed McSparran Hill, Hannah begged for them to stop so she could see the ocean once more. There on the ledge, just past a great square boulder, Hannah rested, staring out at the bay just as she did many times in her youth. The chairmen rotated the litter so that she could get a glimpse of every angle afforded to her from her traveling bed. A servant plucked some flowers growing alongside the great rock and handed them to Hannah, who held them close to her breast.

At length, the sun began to fall under the horizon, and the evening gun from Fort George in Newport Harbor, mixed with the roar of a fern owl, signaled their need to press onward. Mr. Robinson begged that they continue before darkness set in. Hannah was returned to her home, where she passed on October 30, 1773, at the age of twenty-seven. As for Simons, he returned some time later and found that she had died. She was first

Hannah Robinson Ledge on McSparran Hill, although overgrown, still offers a stunning view of the bay.

Hannah Robinson Rock just above the ledge of the same name sits in the woods of Hannah Robinson Park.

The family marker for the Robinsons in Narragansett Historical Cemetery No. 13.

placed in a temporary tomb but was later removed to a special burial place. Peter Simons asked permission to be present for her interment. Rowland Robinson granted his wish but spoke very little with the man, remaining civil to the end.

Rowland Robinson died in 1806, never fully recovering from the death of his daughter. In his book *The History of the Episcopal Church in Narragansett, Rhode Island*, Wilkins Updike presented Rowland Robison as a stubborn, heartless man, yet his accounts and affections speak otherwise. Peter Simons is also portrayed as a villain, yet he may have also been cast in a bad light.

The story here is as told from the writings of the Robinson and Hazard families, along with those of Updike. The Hazards were married into the Robinson family and vice-versa.

A small sentence reveals the other version of the unfortunate Hannah Robinson. J.R. Cole, in telling the tale, ends with, "She expired in her husband's arms." There is record that her husband was not the rogue he is written to be. According to other accounts, they married and stayed married and in love for ten years, until Hannah's untimely death, which may have been from one of the many illnesses that were prevalent of the day. Another not so small detail

The Bowen monument in Acotes Cemetery, where Hannah Simons Bowen, daughter of Hannah Robinson Simons and Peter Simons, is buried.

that may attest to this is that they had a daughter. Hannah Robinson Simons was born on February 19, 1762 (the stone states 1767). She married Dr. Joseph Bowen of Glocester, Rhode Island, on December 12, 1782, in Providence. She died on December 7, 1824, at the age of sixty-two, nine months and eighteen days. Joseph, born in 1756, died on August 12, 1832, at the age of seventy-six. There would later come Hannah Robinson Bowen, born on April 16, 1841, in Glocester, granddaughter of Hannah Robinson Simons Bowen, who was the daughter of Hannah Robinson Simons. Hannah Simons Bowen and her husband, Joseph, carried on the tradition, as did later generations, solidifying the case that Hannah Simons was the daughter of Hannah Robinson.

It seems very strange how the writings never mention Hannah Simons. Could it be that they did not want anyone to know the child? Were they embarrassed by the situation, were they trying to paint a different picture or was it a better tale to tell without mention of the daughter?

Hannah Robinson Simons-Bowen is buried at Acotes Cemetery in Chepachet, Rhode Island, along with her husband, her son and a few other members of the Bowen family. You cannot miss the tall monument at the top of the hill just past the corner.

One more quaint detail came to light while researching the complete story of Hannah Robinson. Dr. Joseph Bowen's father, Colonel Benjamin Bowen, was married twice. His second wife, Abigail, was the mother of Peter Simons, being first married to Peter Simons Sr. Peter Simons Jr. is the father of Hannah, who married Colonel Bowen's son, Joseph. Of course the relation is by marriage.

McSparran Hill, where Hannah played as a child and enjoyed in her last days but for a few moments, is now called Hannah Robinson Park. John Hazard Wells conveyed the land, once part of McSparran Farm, to Preserve Rhode Island in 1966. The 1.52-acre section includes the ledge where Hannah would sit and look out over the Narragansett Bay and Boston Neck; the great rock, now called Hannah Robinson Rock; and a wooden tower rising forty feet into the sky. Legendary writer Howard Phillips Lovecraft once commented on the rock as being "the finest rural prospect I have seen anywhere."

Mariners once used the rock as a land-bound marker. Of course, that was when the area was devoid of trees, as the settlers used wood for the construction of homes and as a source of heat.

THE EAST THOMPSON
STONE CHAMBER

There are enough stone chambers in New England to fill a book on them. In fact, several books have been written regarding these mysterious structures that grace the New England countryside. Many of them sit in backyards or on old farmland, where they now function as storage sheds or root cellars. But that was not the original purpose of these archaeological artifacts. Some remain isolated from modern reconstruction, waiting for someone to decipher the meaning of their original intention. Sitting unassuming in the woods between Thompson Road and the Air Line trail is one such archaeological mystery. The stone chamber in Thompson seems to possess an important link to their origin and use, yet it is barely ever heeded with much concern except by archaeologists and scientists who study such arcane obscurities.

Legend states that the chamber, known as the "Hermit's Cave" to locals, was built by Norsemen who became shipwrecked in Newport. A small band traveled north and settled in present-day Thompson, perhaps for the winter, where they built the chamber for shelter. This could be a valid claim, but there is no known expedition that may have traveled through that particular area, and there were no Viking artifacts ever found that would suggest a sojourn in that place. This shelter took time and effort to build and was carefully erected for a specific purpose.

Another theory is that it was a colonial root cellar, but if one makes a study of root cellars, it must be noted that these chambers do not make proper storage lockers for any type of items that might be fit for human

A view of the east Thompson chamber. This is believed to be part of an extinct Indian prayer village.

A magical moment in the east Thompson stone chamber as the afternoon light flows in.

consumption. Root cellars require ventilation to avoid dampness and mold. They would also need to be built in such a way as to maintain a constant temperature with little variance. The chamber has no door or even marks where one may have once been attached. A door would be vital for ventilation, temperature control and even security against animals.

Most chambers, as in the case of the Thompson chamber, have small entries measuring roughly three feet in height. This would not make a convenient entryway for the farmer to constantly use. It is a good size for keeping wild animals from entering, as witnessed from hiking the Appalachian Trail from Berlin, New Hampshire, to Grafton Notch, Maine. Lean-tos and enclosed shelters are provided roughly every five miles. The Carlo Col shelter had a smaller entry, and its sleeping quarters were elevated for safety from some of the mountain's more aggressive inhabitants.

Many colonial deeds and records show that these chambers were already in existence when the settlers came to clear the land. The ever-frugal Yankees then converted some of these structures for their own personal use or dismantled them completely, unaware of their historic significance. Some sit on properties today outfitted with doors, shelves and even floors (none of the nearly eight hundred known chambers in New England was known to have anything more than a dirt floor). The east Thompson chamber seems to have been untouched by colonial influence.

Another possibility in the long list of builders is the Indians who thrived in the region. James Mavor and Byron Dix, using documentation from early settlers, among other sources, focused on the theory that these chambers were part of a series of Indian prayer villages that stretched into northeastern Connecticut. They did not exclude the possibility that the beehive chamber in Thompson may have been of Irish origin.

The Thompson chamber is a corbelled beehive chamber, with stone slabs placed on one another, overlapping with each successive layer. The result is a beehive- or dome-shaped roof with a capstone. This particular chamber is one of the very few of its kind in New England, yet they are found quite commonly in Ireland. It is one of the largest in New England. Although the entrance of the chamber is constricting, the interior has ample room for people to move about in an upright position. Within the chamber are three triangular stones that graduate in size and are embedded into the wall. Their purpose, if they are more than just support, is at present unknown.

Popular belief is that it was an Indian sweat lodge or ceremonial chamber, yet these types of structures are only found in the east. Whether they are actually Irish or Celtic in origin remains a heated debate among

The interior of the east Thompson chamber. The beehive shape is due to a technique called "corbelling" and is uncommon to such chambers found throughout New England.

scholars. They do seem to protrude from the earth within the vicinities of main watercourses, giving rise to the thought that early explorers used the waterways to travel and built their huts near the rivers for the ease of procuring food and drink. Most major cities are built along the banks of rivers or oceans, so this idea is one of human instinct and not so much the brainchild of theory.

The Thompson chamber is an enigma, as it is not ultimately close to any major tributary, although Long Pond and the Five Mile River are close by, along with the famous Lake Chargoggagoggmanchauggagoggchaubunagungamaugg. They are not considered to be easy to access from the chamber site, as much as the Connecticut River (or the Merrimack River, for example) is a major traveling watercourse.

Vikings, Indians, root cellars, Culdee monks or some other passing civilization are all theories that have been brought forth to solve the mystery of who built this chamber. We do know that the builders were skilled at their art, as the chamber, like so many others, has stood for many centuries if not millennia. It makes you wonder how long that raised ranch that went up on your street not too long ago will last.

Two Taverns in One

Here is a small story containing spirits of a different kind. It is an amusing little account that shows true Yankee ingenuity at its best. Still standing on the Mohegan/Uxbridge line between the states of Rhode Island and Massachusetts is a building that once was a tavern. The property now sits where the old Richardson sawmill is located. The sawmill is still operated by the members of the same family, who have been there for many generations. In fact, the apparatus used to run the mill hails back to times when life was much simpler and less hectic. The mill specializes in the cutting of timber the old-fashioned way for the re-creation or renovation of old homes, having piles of old, wide planks on the premises.

During the days before the American Revolution and shortly after, there sat a tavern on the land. Victual licenses, much like today, varied from town to town and, later, state to state. The owner knew how to get around this little technicality. By having the tavern on the state line, he furnished the building with a mirror-image taproom on either side of the building. When authorities would come to check on his curfew, spies, who were probably paid in libations, would rush ahead and warn the folks drinking after hours. They would then reconvene on the other side of the tavern (in the other state), exempt from the jurisdiction of the approaching authorities. This went on for quite some time until the abutting towns decided that it was time to put a stopper on the matter.

Legislatures took action, and the state boundary was squared off directly around the tavern, putting the whole building in the state of Rhode Island, solely under the jurisdiction of its regulations. Mr. Taylor went back to regular business hours, and in time, new roads with more direct routes to cities and towns outdated the little back road tavern. The square cutout still exists to this day, although on a map, it would not be visible unless greatly magnified.

One more little tidbit. The place was once called Jim Taylor's Roadhouse. An Armenian man was shot and killed by Taylor when he attempted to take one of Taylor's girls, Maggie McNulty. McNulty may have been an employee or Taylor's girlfriend. The legend has never been specific as to her role in the story. Locals say that it is haunted but are not sure of the identity of the ghost.

THE FIRST AIRPLANE STOLEN
IN VERMONT

State Director of Aeronautics Edward F. Knapp said that, so far as he knew, it was the first time an airplane had been stolen in Vermont.

In the early days of aviation, there were many eccentric ideas and inventions. Airplanes were the new frontier, and pilots were the heroes of the sky. Being primitive by today's standards, even in 1948, aircraft were easy to steal—if one was qualified to fly them. Sometimes, however, things did not go as smoothly as planned. This true account took place in Fair Haven, just outside Rutland, Vermont, in October 1948.

Special thanks go out to the *Rutland Herald*, Mickey Kelly, Fred Remington, the Rutland Historical Society and *Sam's Good News* in Rutland for reprinting this next narrative and allowing us to present their account to you. Enjoy.

The headline read, "POLICE STILL IN DARK ABOUT MISSING PLANE STOLEN IN FAIR HAVEN. NO CLUES TO GUIDE SEARCHING FOR PILOT WHO CRASHED ONE PLANE, TOOK OFF IN ANOTHER THURSDAY." The article appeared in the *Rutland Herald* on October 23, 1948, and is quite amusing:

> *Investigators said tonight the trail of the unknown pilot who wrecked one plane and stole another ends where he left the ground at Fair Haven airport.*
> *An all day search of the countryside was made yesterday by pilots from the Rutland and Fair Haven airports without success.*

Civil aeronautics authorities as far south as Washington, D.C., and as far west as Cleveland, Ohio, were put on alert in the search for the missing airplane, and all airfields for a two-hundred-mile radius were asked to have pilots search for the missing flyer.

Richard Hurd, who was the assistant to the state director of aeronautics at the time, flew in from Montpelier to perform an investigation at the field. He took photographs of the wrecked airplane, wheel tracks and the hangar where the plane was taken from and questioned employees and nearby residents. No one had seen any suspicious-looking persons near the field nor were there any motives as to why the plane would have been taken.

State police assisted Hurd by checking present and former students at the field, which was a branch of E.W. Coe's Rutland Flying School. This turned out to be a dead end as well. There was one clue that surfaced during the investigation: a gas station attendant in Fair Haven reported that two young blond men in a blue automobile stopped at his business around 5:00 p.m. and asked for directions to the airfield. Having no knowledge of what was to transpire, the attendant gave directions but never quite got a good look at the two men.

It was surmised that someone familiar with the airfield carried out the theft. State Director of Aeronautics Edward Knapp noted that it was a moonlit night, perfect for flying, and under those conditions, someone who was an experienced pilot could easily fly one to two hundred miles before landing in a field or meadow to refuel. "He may still be in the air somewhere, for all we know," Knapp said.

Knapp also told the press that the position of the ignition switch, when examined by Hurd, indicated that the wrecked aircraft most likely could have been without a pilot when it crashed. The switch was on the left magneto only. If the pilot were ready to start the plane from the cockpit, both left and right magnetos would have been switched. It was assumed that the pilot might have thought that the switch was off and was turning the propeller by hand when the plane started and charged into the shed. The throttle, which was found wide open, could have been thrown into that position by the vibration of the engine and force of the craft lunging forward.

The fact that the planes were on opposite sides of the hangar when it was locked up for the night suggested that the pilot was not familiar with the airfield. After the pilot wrecked the Taylorcraft, he or they had to go through a partition and open another hangar door to get to the second craft, an Aeronca. There was no evidence present to indicate whether one or more persons had taken the aircraft. One person could have easily rolled the planes out of the hangar, started them and lifted away into the night, even though it was noted that both planes could have carried two people.

As of October 25, four days after the plane disappeared, both craft and pilot were still unaccounted for. Police took fingerprints from the wrecked plane and sent them to Montpelier in the hopes of finding a match. The police also took into consideration that the plane may have prearranged a landing place to refuel and took off again. They also brought forth the possibility that the plane landed close to Fair Haven and was in a barn being repainted. Vermont state police trooper Roland Hovey thought that it was more probable that the plane crashed in a desolate area and would not be found for weeks.

On November 11, Hovey's theory was brought to light when the paper printed the news that the plane had been discovered in the woods of a thinly settled section of Glastonbury Mountain by two hunters who stumbled onto the wreckage. There were no bodies found at the crash site. Just when it sounds like it could not get better, the November 13 headline and follow-up article in the *Herald* read:

BELIEVE PHANTOM PILOT RETURNED TO SCENE AFTER SURVIVING CRASH

Vermont's "phantom pilot" who evidently survived the crack up of Glastonbury Mountain of a plane stolen in Fair Haven is a nervy individual who investigators believe returned to "the scene of the crime." Two bits of evidence discovered in a search of the area led them to believe that the thief returned to the wreckage long after he climbed out of the smashed plane.

A repair form was less weather-beaten than it should have been from three weeks exposure. In addition a leather packet, which originally contained the form was found close by the plane under a pile of leaves. The only slight clue to the pilot's identity was a pair of welder's goggles, which E.W. Coe of Rutland, owner of the plane, was unable to account for.

Coe burned the wreckage of his plane yesterday after removing the salvageable parts.

The phantom pilot was never caught, and to this day, as far as anyone knows, it remains a mystery as to who stole the aircraft and why it crashed.

Portsmouth's Strange Discovery

In 2003, Portsmouth, New Hampshire city workers came upon a gruesome discovery while repairing water mains. Several coffins were unearthed from under Chestnut Street. The routine project of digging for the purpose of a manhole became an archaeological dig as teams were brought in to find out who was buried there and why.

Archaeologists removed eight coffins before the work could resume. During the excavations, it was discovered that a sewer line had been laid straight through some of the burials. These eight coffins were just the tip of the iceberg. Eighteen individuals were soon extracted from under the city street. DNA testing of the first eight found confirmed that they were four African males, one female, one juvenile and two others of undetermined age and sex.

The city had found what was once thought to be a legend, the lost "Negro Burial Ground" that appeared on a 1705 city map but had vanished from subsequent maps in the nineteenth century. The burial ground contained roughly two hundred burials that were once located on the outskirts of the town but now lay underneath its streets and buildings. An 1813 map of the town shows buildings and streets where the burial ground once was.

This burial ground is the oldest of its kind in the northern portion of New England. At some point, it was encroached on, presumably intentional as city officials had to be aware of its presence. The people who were buried there were placed in wooden coffins and buried with great care, most likely having proper burial markers put in place at each grave.

African Burial Ground Memorial in Portsmouth, where an estimated two hundred African Americans may be buried under the streets and buildings.

One of the many plaques along the Black Heritage Trail in Portsmouth telling a short history of the area where the African Burial Ground is contained.

There were stories and legends of a possible burial ground once occupying that particular area, but it was widely believed to be legend by many and not much more. In fact, it was just a popular belief that the Portsmouth Music Hall was built over a portion of the old burial ground. Of course, this was considered an old wives' tale until the historical discovery.

The Portsmouth Black Heritage Society was well aware of the lost burial ground and history of African Americans in the city. In 2000, the society installed a bronze plaque near the site marking the existence of the burial ground. There is also a Black Heritage Trail adorned with plaques on the sides of buildings offering historical tidbits about the history of the area. As of this writing, plans are underway to complete a memorial park in honor of those buried in the cemetery under the city.

The exact number of burials may forever remain a mystery unless the city wants to start excavating streets and cellars within the vicinity of the old burial ground—a venture that would put a more accurate number on the burials but at the same time turn downtown into a "big dig" for an inestimable amount of time. The memorial park seems like a more reasonable compromise for the time being. At least the people of Portsmouth have knowledge of the burial ground's existence and can take measures to preserve a piece of history that has surfaced in a most peculiar way.

In the case of Portsmouth's burial ground, one legend has been laid to rest while another is just beginning.

Bailey's Mills/Spite Cemetery

One of our favorite legends of New England takes place in the small village of Reading, Vermont, just southeast of Rutland. If you travel down a small gravel road called Bailey's Mills Road, you will come to a building now used as a bed-and-breakfast. The home came into the possession of the innkeeper Barbara Thaeder's family in the mid-1960s and has been a bed-and-breakfast for many years. The small road travels directly in front of the house as it laces through the narrow valley. In the winter, it is not advisable to travel the road any farther than the Bailey's Mills front door. As you pull up to the front door, another strange sight will catch your eye. The Bailey's Mills Bed-and-Breakfast has the exquisite distinction of having a cemetery in its front yard. Although this may not be out of the ordinary in New England, the name of the cemetery and the reason for it being there is a tale for the telling.

Levi Bailey (1766–1850) purchased the dam and mill in 1794. Between 1800 and his death in 1850, the enterprise prospered, and Bailey continued to expand his industrial complex until the land held a three-story woolen factory, several other mills, a blacksmith shop and a company store. Employees of the complex lived in a brick house and bought their goods at the company store, no doubt giving Bailey a chance to recoup his wages paid out—at a profit, no less.

In 1808, Bailey sought to expand beyond his property to a lot across the small lane that was then a state road. His closest neighbor, David Hapgood, owned the land. Levi asked in good faith to purchase the piece of property

A wonderful view of Bailey's Mills Bed-and-Breakfast, with Spite Cemetery in the front yard.

that lay just across the street from his, but Hapgood, who was irritated by the mere sight of Bailey, outright refused.

Bailey would not give up that easily, but his persistence was met with harsh refusal to sell the valuable parcel. As time wore on, Bailey began to resent his neighbor and at one point yelled over to the man that he would soon die, and when he did, Bailey would have his lot. Hapgood, knowing this to be true, made arrangements for the land in such a way that his nemesis would never acquire it. He gave it to the town for use as a burial ground. To make matters more infuriating to Bailey, when John Hapgood died in 1829, he was among the first to be buried in the cemetery. Every morning, Bailey would tend to his businesses with the stone of his archenemy in life sitting spitefully on the land he would never have. For this reason, the burial ground is now called Spite Cemetery, but this is not the end of the story.

Levi Bailey was not a man to give up so easily. He also purchased a burial plot for his family in the cemetery, and when he died on October 21, 1850, at the age of eighty-five, he was buried right near his neighbor. It seemed that Bailey was also able to spite Hapgood, as he did acquire the land he so desired, although not as much, and for eternity instead.

Left: The stone and plot of David Hapgood in Spite Cemetery.

Below: Levi Bailey's timeworn stone in Spite Cemetery.

Barbara Thaeder is not sure how long Levi Bailey actually lived in her home due to the fact that he built a beautiful mansion just up the road a ways on a hill overlooking the valley. The Hapgood home still stands across the road from the cemetery. The river runs by the bed-and-breakfast, and the remains of the dam and mills can still be spied along the property. The road now serves as more of a drive-through and shortcut through a field as it makes its way up the hill toward more populated areas.

The general store is now a museum re-creation of what it may have looked like in Bailey's time. There is a legend that is told on the bed-and-breakfast's website of a boy who entered the store with a shiny new penny looking to purchase something. The young man scoured the stock looking for the best deal he could find for his coin. He finally came upon the barrel of figs, whereupon he pulled out the biggest of the lot. Old man Bailey took the penny and examined the fig. He decided that it was much too big a piece of produce for the price of a penny and proceeded to take a bite out of the fig before handing the uneaten portion to the astonished child.

Lovecraft and New England

Legends are born every minute, but many do not receive the recognition they wholly deserve. New England is full of great authors who have passed on, but their works still live as testaments to their talents and imagination. One particular author, although world-renowned, seems in many cases to have been forgotten in his hometown, let alone New England, where the region became his playground for the settings of his stories. That man is Howard Phillips Lovecraft.

If you wander through his home city of Providence, Rhode Island, you will not see a Lovecraft history trail nor the buildings he lived in marked—in fact, some have been torn down. There are no plaques on the homes and streets he used in his stories (save but one on the lawn of the John Hay Library). It is as if the man was as fictional as his work. There is a gravestone, although it is hardly enough to commemorate a man who traveled the region and, being enlightened by its wonder, used many places as the background for his stories.

Howard Phillips Lovecraft was born on August 20, 1890, in his home at 194 Angell Street in Providence, Rhode Island. Lovecraft was a precocious young man—some say even a genius. In 1893, his father, Winfield Scott Lovecraft, was committed to Butler Hospital for acute mental illness, and he remained there until his death in 1898. During this period, young Howard's mother, two aunts and his grandfather, Whipple Van Buren Phillips, raised him. Lovecraft, being feeble of health from birth, was not able to attend school until he was eight years old. Even that only lasted about one year,

Above: The John Hay Library in Providence, Rhode Island's East Side, where the Lovecraft memorial plaque sits.

Left: The memorial plaque to Howard Phillips Lovecraft on the lawn of the John Hay Library on Providence, Rhode Island's East Side.

although later he would attend Hope High School in Providence. He completed his studies but never received his diploma for his efforts. He spent much of his youth at the Ladd Observatory on Hope Street in his home city, studying astronomy and chemistry. At age nine, he became a published writer, having several hectographed publications in the *Scientific Gazette*. Lovecraft had already shown his prodigious abilities at age three by reciting poetry and later writing his own. One of his main early influences was his grandfather, who promoted his reading and writing until his death in 1904.

Although the family was well off, ill health and bad financial administration chipped away at the family wealth. His mother was committed to Butler Hospital in 1919 and died on May 24, 1921, of complications from gall bladder surgery. By then, Lovecraft had published his first fictional works, starting in 1919 with *The Vagrant*. This would be the beginning of a long succession of fictional works by the author that would be published in various magazines. Unfortunately, Lovecraft never thought of himself as a major-league writer, and he continued to submit his work to pulp magazines, primarily *Weird Tales*, for small pittances that barely paid his expenses.

During this period in his life, he kept in close correspondence with his fans and those he had befriended in the business. It is estimated that he wrote about 100,000 letters to the various people with whom he stayed in close communication.

Lovecraft was married for a short time to Sonia Greene, who was seven years older than he. They moved to Brooklyn, New York, where they stayed until financial difficulties forced his wife to relocate to Cleveland. Lovecraft stayed in New York for a brief time but yearned for his hometown Providence.

The couple agreed to divorce but never finalized the act. Lovecraft moved back to his hometown, where he lived with his aunts the remainder of his life. From 1933 until his death from intestinal cancer on March 15, 1937, Lovecraft wrote some of his greatest work and even worked as a ghostwriter for people such as close friend and colleague C.M. Eddy and Harry Houdini. In his last year, he lived in constant pain from the cancer, keeping a dairy of his illness. Lovecraft was buried in the Phillips plot at Swan Point Cemetery. In 1977, a group of fans raised enough funds to have a special headstone put in place at his grave. The headstone is inscribed with his name, dates of birth and death and the phrase, "I AM PROVIDENCE," part of a quote from his personal letters, where he stated, "I am Providence, and Providence is myself."

Every year around the anniversary of his death, Lovecraft aficionados Keith and Carl Johnson hold a tribute to the author at the Ladd Observatory on Hope

Note the inscription on Lovecraft's stone: "I AM PROVIDENCE."

The Ladd Observatory in Providence, Rhode Island, is where H.P. Lovecraft spent much time during his youth.

Street in Providence. There is always a healthy throng of "Lovecraftians" in attendance to pay homage to the legend through poems, readings and song. After the tribute, a visit to the Phillips plot rounds out a well-deserved acknowledgment to one of New England's greatest writers.

To say that the influence New England had on Lovecraft and the influence Lovecraft had on New England were exceedingly great would be understatements. Every new journey through New England opened up a new chapter in his work. Following are some of the places that are either mentioned in his works, which number over one hundred stories, or are the main locations for his tales.

Pascoag and Chepachet, Rhode Island, are mentioned from the first paragraph of *The Horror at Red Hook*, written in 1925 and published in *Weird Tales* in January 1927. *Herbert West, Reanimator* (1922) and *The Case of Charles Dexter Ward* (1933) take place in Providence. In fact, the address mentioned in the latter story, 10 Barnes Street, was a home Lovecraft resided in at one point. The former also mentions Boston, Massachusetts, as does *Pickman's Model* (1926) and *The Street* (1919).

Vermont is the setting for *A Whisperer in the Darkness* (1930), along with the lighthearted *Sweet Ermengarde*. *The Dunwich Horror* (1928) takes place in central Massachusetts, although the fictional town of Arkham is also mentioned. Many believe that this place was based on Salem, Massachusetts. Arkham is used in many of his writings, as is Miskatonic University. Innsmouth and Kingsport were names given in stories after his visits to Newburyport and Marblehead. Haverhill seems to be a favorite hometown for some of his characters. *The Unnamable* (1923) mentions a willow in an old burial ground in Salem. This is the spitting image of the great tree that sits in the middle of the Charter Street Burying Point in Salem. The mausoleum described in *The Tomb* (1917) resembles one set back in a hill hidden by tall overgrowth at Providence's Swan Point Cemetery, where Lovecraft is buried.

Of course, *The Shunned House* (1924) takes place on Providence's East Side and also mentions Exeter, Rhode Island, while the main scene mentioned in *In the Vault* (1925) resembles a mixture of Chestnut Hill Cemetery in Exeter and perhaps another place he had visited—at least that is what I imagined upon reading the story.

Newport, Rhode Island; Bolton, Massachusetts; Brattleboro, Vermont; and a host of other New England towns and cities grace the pages of Lovecraft's tales of the wild and weird. These are just a few of the examples of how Lovecraft may be more than just Providence. Perhaps it would suffice to make an addendum to the phrase on his stone to say, "I AM NEW ENGLAND."

As a treat to Lovecraft fans and those about to become ones, I would like to offer the opening greeting spoken at the annual H.P. Lovecraft Tribute Services in Swan Point Cemetery by Carl L. Johnson. Officially, H.P. Lovecraft was his second cousin, twice removed. His mother's maiden name is Beverly D. Place. She, and therefore Keith and Carl Johnson, are related to Robey Place, who married Whipple Van Buren Philips. While they resided on a farm in Foster, Rhode Island, they had two children. Their second child, a daughter, was named Sarah Susan Lovecraft. This was Howard Phillips Lovecraft's mother. They are also related to the Lovecrafts through the Frys and Phillips family lines.

Both H.P. Lovecraft and Carl's family are descended from Roger Williams, founder of the city of Providence, Rhode Island. He was not aware of the familial connection to H.P. Lovecraft until the time he was organizing the first public H.P. Lovecraft Service of Tribute, which was conducted on Sunday, March 15, 1987—the fiftieth anniversary of the author's passing—at the Lovecraft grave site within the Phillips family plot in Swan Point Cemetery, 585 Blackstone Boulevard, Providence, Rhode Island. To promote the occasion, Carl conducted research for an article in the local periodical, *East Side Monthly*. In one of the biographies Carl read—*Lovecraft*, by L. Sprague DeCamp—to his surprise (and delight), he discovered some hints of connections to H.P. Lovecraft. Even with modest notice, one hundred persons attended that first tribute service. Here is Carl's opening speech:

Swan Point is a quiet, picturesque cemetery situated in the northern reach of Providence, Rhode Island's East Side, overlooking the Seekonk River. It is renowned for the many, extraordinary sculptures and serves as the final resting place for noted American statesmen, soldiers and governors. Monuments erected in enduring tribute to Rhode Island's societal architects and to titans of the Industrial Age loom impressively over an array of polished marble, granite and alabaster stones. For this historic splendor, however, there is one section of the two hundred acre expanse, which seems to attract considerably more attention and draw more visitors than the rest, particularly during the middle of March and the end of October.

This is the Phillips plot wherein repose the mortal remains of the much acclaimed writer of horror fiction, Howard Phillips Lovecraft, born August 20, 1890, died March 15, 1937. Maps tracing the route to the plot are available at the Cemetery's office. Mr. Lovecraft was born in Rhode Island's capitol city one hundred and nineteen years ago, and died there five months shy of his forty-seventh birthday, nearly impoverished with he and an aunt having less than $500 expected to sustain them for the rest of their lives, and disenfranchised, believing himself to have been a failure at writing, at least as having achieved any commercial practicality. He left behind a small circle of loyal friends and correspondents. Yet today, he is considered by many avid readers to be the peer of Edgar Allan Poe, whom he had revered. He has also been referred to as, "the Stephen King of the earlier twentieth century." Thursday, March 15, 2012 will mark the 75th anniversary of H.P. Lovecraft's passing.

H.P. Lovecraft has been established as an important figure in American literature, and his fame in the annals of horror fiction endures. In the decades since his death, the very name of Lovecraft has become synonymous with gripping, supernatural suspense, and his devotees throughout America, Great Britain and Europe continue to gather in celebration of his literary legacy. One such event is the annual _Necronomicon_, which is a horror fiction hobnobber with Lovecraft motif held in various cities throughout the U.S. The name is a play on a Lovecraft story line, referring to the Necronomicon. His stories evince his unique capacity to invoke a reader's innate dread of the unknown—or, "UNNAMED"—of other-worldly forces which might be lurking beneath the surface of the earth, within subterranean caverns, beyond the clouds, from an alien star system, behind the eyes of a stranger, or that most oppressive fear of having to doubt one's own perception of reality!

As chilling and penetrating as are his writings, H.P. Lovecraft avowed that he embraced no belief whatsoever in the supernatural, including anything which smacked of spiritualism. He dismissed astrology as, "an appalling and frivolous pseudo-science." Lovecraft thoroughly prided himself on his sense of the rational and apparent. One of H.P. Lovecraft's closest friends and writing colleagues, Frank Belknap Long, stated in his biography of Lovecraft, Dreamer on the Night Side (published by Arkham House Publishing Co., 1975), that, "Lovecraft was an extreme 'scientific materialist.' He had no patience with anything that went contrary to what modern biochemistry or astrophysics or any other branch of science has revealed about the nature of the universe, or life on this planet." This rational outlook could have provided emotional grounding during the more trying circumstances to which he was subjected.

The sole offspring of an old and fading New England family, young Howard was raised with an illusion of their former affluence. An unusually precocious child, he could write at the age of three and by age eight, he was busy composing little stories! Howard combed the treasures contained in *his Grandfather Phillips' expansive personal library; some of his earliest reading included 1001 Arabian Knights. For a time, the boy Lovecraft was walking about with a towel wrapped about his pate, calling himself "Abdul Alhazred," seeker of forbidden truths and arcane literature! (This character would later emerge in Lovecraft's writings as "the Mad Arab" who in the ninth century uncovered the Necronomicon, or Book of the Dead, a fictional, nefarious tome containing forbidden incantations and sigils.) His father, Winfield Scott Lovecraft, was a traveling sales representative for the Gorham & Gorham Silver Company. He suffered a nervous collapse in 1893, quite possibly brought about by protracted syphilis which had too long gone untreated. Shortly thereafter, Mr. Lovecraft was confined to Butler Psychiatric Hospital in Providence, not far from their home, and succumbed to his malady at the facility five years later. When Howard's maternal grandfather Whipple Van Buren Phillips died in 1904, the family moved out of their spacious, Victorian manse at 454 Angel Street and relocated to a more modest dwelling down the street at 588 Angel, corner of Butler Avenue. Two decades later, Howard would again reside there with his two aunts on the mother's side, Lillian Clark and Annie Gamwell.*

Howard Lovecraft's mother, Sarah Susan "Susie" Lovecraft, became neurotically protective of her son, dressing him in girlish attire until his fifth year, which was, however, not so very unusual for that time, and making efforts to convince the child that he should avoid the company of others, due to his "homeliness." (Photographs of her son in early youth do not support this motherly opinion!) Herself committed to Butler Hospital in 1919, from where she would not emerge in life, Sarah Susan Lovecraft dies in a state of profound dementia in 1921.

Later in 1924, H.P. married Sonia Haft Greene to whom he had been introduced at a Boston literary soirée several years before. Sonia was a Jewish, Russian immigrant seven years older than Howard. Their wedding vows were exchanged in a church in Brooklyn, New York. The marriage was dissolved following a two years residence in New York, during which span H.P. struggled to secure steady employment, continued his writing, yet pined increasingly to return home to his beloved Providence, Rhode Island.

H.P. Lovecraft was a prodigious letter writer, maintaining a voluminous flow of correspondence and authoring over 100,000 missives. Many of those were dozens of pages in length, written in long-hand and illustrated with his own drawings.

A chronic insomniac, Lovecraft by night walked the darkening streets of Providence (alluded to in some of his fiction as, the "Ancient Hill"),

Boston, or Gotham, garnering inspiration for his haunting short stories and novellas which were published in the pulp magazines popular in his time and up to the 1950s, the best remembered of these being Hugo Gernsback's {Experimental Publishing} Amazing Stories and J.C. Henneberger's Weird Tales. A unique mythology of Lovecraft's own invention eventually emerged through his stories, and this was dubbed (plus utilized) by Lovecraft's admiring inner circle of writers as his "C'Thulhu Mythos." C'thulhu was a monstrous, squid/octopus creature of extraterrestrial origins, who had been vanquished by the "Elder Gods" as interpreted by our distant ancestors in a remote age, Great C'thulhu "sleeps" in a subterranean cavern, biding his time until the stars display a certain alignment and his ministers on earth call him to the surface, that he shall regain his dominion!

At least ten of Lovecraft's works, including Pickman's Model, The Dunwich Horror, The Terror, The Shuttered Room, Cool Air, Dagon, and Herbert West: Reanimator have been translated to the feature movie or television screen, albeit with some interpretation. Several years ago there was discussion of a movie about Lovecraft's life, which was scripted but not produced. Actor Johnny Depp was considered for the role of H.P. Lovecraft, and Christina Ricci was to have portrayed his Russian-American wife Sonia. The author's somewhat reclusive life in Providence and his mercurial writing career were the subjects of an original play by Brett Rutherford of New York, now residing in Providence, entitled Night Gaunts, which was first performed on March 18, 1988 in the historic Providence Athenaeum, a library once frequented By Edgar Allan Poe himself during Poe's courtship of poetess Sarah Helen Whitman. (Unfortunately, it seemed that H.P. Lovecraft was unable to afford the Library's membership dues!)

Lovecraft died from complications of abdominal cancer and resultant nefritis [sic], in relative literary obscurity, five months short of his forty-seventh birthday. His grave, situated next to those of his parents, was left unmarked for four decades, until 1977 when a dedicated group of aficionados contributed their resources to purchase the stone which now rests above him. It is a modest, wedge-shaped block of granite bearing the name Howard Phillips Lovecraft, dates of his birth and death, under which is inscribed the now well-known quote excised from one of his personal correspondences (to Providence neighbor Helen Sulley): I AM PROVIDENCE.

A service of tribute recognizing the unique literary contributions is scheduled to take place on Sunday, April 1, 2012 on the grounds of Ladd Observatory, 210 Doyle Avenue at the corner of Hope Street, Providence strat time of 3 p.m. Since the first such occasion presented as a remembrance of the 50th anniversary of Lovecraft's untimely death on March 15, 1987, the annual event has become something of a Providence tradition and typically draws attendance of approximately 150 persons.

Something out of the ordinary, shall we say, always seems to occur at the annual tributes organized by the H.P. Lovecraft Commemoratives Activities Committee and conducted in recognition to the life and literary legacy of H.P. Lovecraft, often involving a sudden and inexplicable change in weather conditions. Once, for instance, unanticipated snow flurries fell, despite the bright sunshine, for the precise duration of a dirge being sung by an attractive, young woman clad in a black velvet hooded cloak. Murders of crows have been known to light in the leafless branches of nearby trees, and commenced their cacophonous cawing in sync with offered readings of selections from Lovecraft's prose. Strange, cloudy distortions have sometimes appeared in photographs taken at these services originally held within Swan Point. Maybe the presiding shade of H.P. Lovecraft was in its own way letting the gathering known of his bemusement at all the fuss and clamor concerning him, by augmenting the proceedings. But that is mere speculation, and of a decidedly unscientific nature!

Carl would know this as well as anyone, being related to the great writer—not to mention his work in the field of demonology, the paranormal and cryptozoology. I guess such talent does run in the family.

The Capture of Annawon

King Philip's War was one of the bloodiest wars ever fought on American soil. Although the battle lasted for one year and two months, its toll was devastating on the colonists and especially the Indians. Unlike most wars, women and children were mercilessly executed on both sides when whole villages were raided. This was not a war fought for power as much as it was for revenge and obliteration of a culture.

Historians agree that the key factor leading up to the war was the murder of "praying Indian" John Sassamon. "Praying Indians" was the name given to Native American Christian converts. Sassamon, a liaison between the English and the natives, was found murdered in Assawompset Pond. Three Wampanoags were arrested, tried, convicted and hanged for the deed on June 8, 1675. This set off a chain of events by the tribe in retaliation for the English infringing on their sovereignty.

On June 24, 1675, the border town of Swansea was attacked by Indians and, within five days, burned. Fury spread through the colonies as attacks mounted until the English officially declared war on the Wampanoags on September 9, 1675. Some tribes and colonists tried to remain neutral in the skirmish, such as the Rhode Island colony and the Narragansetts, but the tides of war eventually sucked them in.

For the next year, villages from both sides blazed with the glow of fire and death as the warriors and militia battled and retaliated against one another. Metacom—or King Philip, as the English called him—was eventually killed by one of his own, John Alderman, on August 12, 1676, effectively

Anawan Rock in Rehoboth, Massachusetts, is where Annawon and his band were captured on August 28, 1676, effectively ending King Philip's War. This view is the rear of the rock as it faces Route 44. This view is also likely where Annawon was positioned at the time of his capture.

putting an end to the war. But there were still two major players on the side of the Indians who were at large and wreaking havoc on the English: Chief Tisquapin and Philip's second in command, Annawon (also spelled Anawan). The battle in the swamp where Philip was killed would have a major significance.

Captain Benjamin Church, an accomplished Indian fighter, was given the orders to track down Annawon, who had safely fled the skirmish where Philip met his end. Annawon was an older man revered for his bravery and accomplishments in battle under Philip and his father, Chief Massasoit. It was known that Annawon had made it clear that he would not be taken alive by the English, and therefore, Church knew that he would have to create an effective strategy to beat the great warrior, who was now chief.

News traveled that Annawon was held up somewhere in Rehoboth raiding neighboring farms for food. Rehoboth was established in 1643 as part of the Plymouth Colony. Its boundaries were large and included Rumford and Cumberland, Rhode Island. The English, while searching for Annawon, came upon some Indians skinning a horse. They captured them with no resistance thanks to the help of a scout who had come over to the side of the English. The ten men were brought to an old fort, where they were told that siding with Church would spare their lives. This, they decided, was a good idea and asked for their families to be gathered and brought to them. The ten had been part of Annawon's camp sent forth to gather provisions. They had been with Annawon the day before but knew not where he would have "kenneled" at present.

Based on the information gathered from his captives, Church set forth with a small band consisting of just six other men (one white and five Indians) to find the warrior chief. As they approached a swamp, they spied an old man with a rifle slung over his shoulder and a young squaw. The old man was part of Annawon's council, and the young woman was his daughter. They were sent to find the ten men who had gone for provisions. Church informed the man that they were safe in captivity and that his life would also be spared if the two cooperated.

When questioned, both gave the same answers: Annawon and about fifty or sixty men were encamped in Squannakonk Swamp. When asked how many miles the swamp lay from their present position, the squaw answered that she did not know how to measure miles but that the swamp sat a good day's hike ahead. Church then inquired if they could make the swamp by nightfall, and the man answered that they could if they traveled steadfast and stoutly. Church then decided that he would pay Annawon a "visit" despite his small band. The two captives had no choice but to agree to take the Englishman to Annawon.

On August 28, after miles of trudging through brush and mire, the group came upon the area where Annawon and his men kenneled. Their camp was on the edge of a great rock, twenty-five feet tall and seventy-five feet wide. The old man cautioned them to wait until dark, as Annawon sent his scouts out at that time to make sure that there were no enemies about. After the last rays of daylight were well below the horizon, and the scouts had returned to camp, the men carefully proceeded. Church asked the old man if he would fight on his side. The old man begged Church not to make him take arms against his friend but then said, "I will go along with you, and be helpful to you, and shall lay hands upon any man that shall offer hurt to you."

As they approached, they heard the pounding of a stone. It was an Indian woman pounding corn into meal. Church stealthily crept over the rock with the old man and his daughter, and at one point, he could almost touch Annawon. Annawon was resting with his son, both lying in opposite directions. He noted that the men were broken into three companies and that Annawon had used a felled tree lined with brush as cover. Their weapons, close to Annawon's feet, were leaning against a forked branch, with a mat placed over them to protect the flintlocks from dampness or dew. If wet or damp, the powder would not ignite, and the guns would not fire. Church realized that it would be almost impossible to mount an attack from his position. He asked the man if there was any other way in. The man told him that there was no other way in and that his warriors were requested to enter the camp by that way only, as anyone entering from any other direction would immediately be shot.

The men quietly retreated and came up with a new plan. The old man and his daughter set forth, with Church and his men crouching behind them. When the woman pounded corn, the party moved; when she stopped, they would halt their advance. The trail ended by the side of Annawon. The man and woman passed through with no event, and then Church leaped out from behind them, stepping over Annawon's son's head and taking position in front of the makeshift garrison of weapons. Annawon, both surprised and astonished, yelled in a deep, commanding voice, "Howoh!" Several contemporary texts state that the word means, "I am taken," but a translation by Roger Williams, who actually traded and conversed with them regularly, noted it as meaning, "Who is that?" This would make more sense, as he was at first startled by Church.

Church, taking their guns, demanded their surrender, promising them safe passage to Plymouth, where they would be spared. He instructed his scouts to go to the other two companies and tell them the same. The other companies also surrendered without a fight. At that time, Church kept up a ruse that a great army sat waiting in the swamp just outside the camp's firelight. Little did the Indians know that there were only seven men against the encampment of fifty or sixty Wampanoags.

The captain and his men had not slept in two days and had little to no provisions. Church said to Annawon, "I am come to sup with you." Then he asked what they had for supper. Annawon answered in a strong voice, "Taubut," meaning, according to Roger Williams, "It is satisfactory."

Annawon then asked if Church would prefer horse-beef or cow-beef. Church told him that he preferred cow-beef. They supped together on beef and mashed green corn lightly seasoned with salt, which the captain had brought along with him as one of the very few provisions in his possession. After supper was ended, Church asked his men if he might have the opportunity to nap for a few hours while they stood guard over the prisoners; then they would be able to sleep the rest of the night. Sleep did not come to the captain, as his eyes would not close. He sat up and noticed that Annawon was also awake. The two stared at each other for about an hour, not speaking, as Church did not know the Indian language and feared that Annawon knew none of his tongue.

At length, Annawon rose, threw off his blanket and proceeded into the woods. Church did not call out for fear of being thought of as apprehensive. He then thought that perhaps the warrior had a rifle hidden in the brush and began to crouch close to the young son of Annawon in order to shield himself from possible danger. Annawon returned with a bundle in his arms and, unwrapping it, said to Church, "Great captain, you have killed Philip and conquered his country, for I believe, that I and my company are the last that war against the English, so I suppose the war is ended by your means; and therefore, these things belong unto you."

Contained within were the royal accoutrements that Philip donned when sitting in state: the Wampanoag belt adorned with black-and-white beads fashioned into figures, flowers and wild beasts; another smaller belt with flags; and a small belt with a star. All three were edged with red hair from the heads of the Mohawks. There were also two fine horns of glazed powder and a red blanket. The large belt, when placed over Church, stretched from his shoulder to his ankles front and back. These had been passed from Philip to Annawon, who would be the next chief. The two spent the rest of the night sharing stories of their victories and exploits as warriors.

In the morning, they proceeded to march to Plymouth. Church had promised Annawon's men that their lives would be spared but could not offer Annawon the same treatment, as he could not speak for his masters at Plymouth. He told Annawon that he would do everything in his power to beg his superiors to spare the warrior's life. While the rest of the prisoners were brought directly to Plymouth, Annawon and a few of his close scouts were taken to Rhode Island with Church to reside at his home for a few days before proceeding to Plymouth.

Church was then ordered away to capture Chief Tisquapin and his small band, who were raiding farms and killing livestock and horses for food. After his capture, Church traveled to Boston. Upon returning to Plymouth, he became bitterly outraged at what he beheld. On the hill above the village were the heads of Tisquapin and Annawon, suspended from poles for all to see. It is told that Tisquapin claimed that balls from a flintlock could not harm him, but when they tested his assertion, he fell dead from the first shot. Annawon was executed for brutality against the English, which he freely admitted. More than likely, they were facing execution anyway for being ringleaders in the war.

Skirmishes carried on in Maine until a treaty was signed in April 1878 at Casco Bay, effectively ending King Philip's War in the north.

The spirits of those who supposedly lost their lives during a battle that never took place (at what is called Anawan Rock) are reputed to haunt the encampment where Annawon was captured. Visitors to the rock have heard the word "Iootash" (Algonquian for "Stand and fight") reverberate through the sparse woods. The only problem with this claim is that there was no fight for anyone to yell the phrase. In Church's book, he stated that during the battle in the swamps near Mount Hope where Philip was slain, he heard a gruff voice shouting, "Iootash! Iootash!" several times. The actual meaning is vague in the English language, but it can be translated as a verb in the second person meaning, "Fight." Whoever first made this claim for the rock most likely did not study their swamps very well.

Church did not know that it was Annawon at the time until he asked his Indian assistant, Peter, who the man was and what he was saying. Peter related that it was Philip's great captain and that the word meant for the men to stand to it and fight stoutly. Church described Annawon as an "old furly fellow."

Regarding the other supernatural occurrences at the rock, some have even seen shadows flit about the brush as if warriors from long ago were once again scouting the area for the enemy. The smell of campfire smoke and, in some cases, the glow of a campfire are among other occurrences at the rock. Others have experienced time slips and objects being moved. Numerous witnesses believe that the spirits of the Indians, perhaps even Annawon, have returned to reconsider their decision to surrender so easily and actually stand and fight.

Bibliography

Abbott, Katharine M. *Old Paths and Legends of New England*. New York: G.P. Putnam and Sons, 1907.

Adams, Charles Francis. *Massachusetts, Its Historians and Its History*. Boston: Houghton, Mifflin and Company, 1898.

Arnold, James. *Vital Records of Rhode Island*. Providence, RI: Narragansett Historical Publishing Company, 1892.

Blake, Francis Everett. *History of the Town of Princeton in the County of Worcester and the Commonwealth of Massachusetts, 1759–1915*. Vol. 1. Princeton, MA: published by the town, 1915.

Bolte, Mary, and Mary Eastman. *Haunted New England*. Riverside, CT: Chatham Press Inc., 1972.

Bonfanti, Leo. *Strange Beliefs, Customs & Superstitions of New England*. Wakefield, MA: Pride Publications, 1980.

Botkin, B.A. *A Treasury of New England Folklore*. New York: Crown Publisher, 1944.

Cahill, Robert Ellis. *New England's Ancient Mysteries*. Salem, MA: Old Saltbox Publishing House Inc., 1993.

————. *New England's Ghostly Haunts*. Peabody, MA: Chandler-Smith Publishing House Inc., 1983.

Church, Benjamin, Henry Martyn Dexter and Thomas Church. *The History of King Philip's War*. Boston: John Kimball Wiggins, 1865.

Church, Thomas, and Samuel G. Drake. *The History of King Philip's War*. Boston: Howe and Norton, 1825.

Citro, Joseph A. *Cursed in New England*. Guilford, CT: Globe Pequot Press, 2004.

Clauson, James Earl. *These Plantations*. Providence, RI: E.A. Johnson Company, 1937.

Cole, J.R. *History of Washington and Kent Counties, Rhode Island*. New York: W.W. Preston and Company, 1889.

Cornell, John, Reverend, MA. *Geneology of the Cornell Family*. New York: T.A. Wright, 1902.

Daggett, John, and Amelia Daggett Sheffield. *A Sketch of the History of Attleborough from Its Settlement to Its Division*. Boston: Samuel Usher, 1894.

Drake, Samuel Adams. *A Book of New England Legends and Folklore in Prose and Poetry*. Boston: Little, Brown and Company, 1910.

————. *The Border Wars of New England*. New York: Charles Scribner's Sons, 1910.

Folsom, George. *History of Saco and Biddeford, with Notices of Other Early Settlements, and of the Proprietary Government, in Maine, Including the Provinces of New Somersetshire and Lygonia*. Saco, ME: Alex C. Putnam, 1830.

Granite 13, no. 1 (January 1903). A.M. Boston, Hunt and Company.

Hare, Augustus J.C. *Epitaphs for Country Churchyards*. Oxford, UK: John Henry and James Parker, 1856.

Hayward, John. *The New England Gazetteer*. Concord, NH: Israel S. Boyd and William White, 1829.

Hazard, Thomas Robinson, and Rowland Gibson. *The Johnny-Cake Papers of "Sheperd Tom," Together with Reminiscences of Narragansett Schools of Former Days*. Boston: printed by subscriber, 1915.

Hazard, Thomas Robinson, and Willis Pope. *Recollections of Olden Times*. Newport, RI: John F. Sanborn, 1879.

Hosmer, James Kendall. *Winthrop's Journal: "History of New England."* Vols. 1 and 2. New York: Charles Scribner's Sons, 1908.

Johnson, Clifton. *What They Say in New England: A Book of Signs, Sayings, and Superstitions*. Boston: Lee and Shepard Publishers, 1896.

Leonard, Mary Hall. *Mattapoisett and Old Rochester*. New York: Grafton Press, 1907.

Lincoln, Allen B. *A Modern History of Windham County, Connecticut*. Vol. 2. Chicago: S.J. Clarke Publishing Company, 1920.

Lodi, Edward. *Witches of Plymouth County and Other New England Sorceries*. Middleborough, MA: Rock Village Publishing, 2004.

Macek, Paul J., and James R. Morrison. *Early History of Webster, Dudley and Oxford*. Webster, MA: self-published, 2000.

Matthews, Margery. *Peleg's Last Word: The Story of The Foster Woolen Manufactory*. North Scituate, RI: Cardinal Press, 1987.

Mavor, James W., and Byron E. Dix. *Manitou: The Sacred Landscape of New England's Native Civilization*. Rochester, VT: Inner Traditions International Ltd., 1989.

Norman, Michael, and Beth Scott. *Haunted Historic America*. New York: Tom Doherty Associates LLC, 1995.

Nutting, George M. *Massachusetts: A Guide to Its Places and People*. Cambridge, MA: Riverside Press, 1937.

Olcott, Henry S. *People from the Other World*. Hartford, CT: American Publishing Company, 1875.

Old Rhode Island Magazine 2, no. 9 (October 1992). Nostalgia Publishing Inc.

Perry, Amos. *Rhode Island State Census, 1885*. Providence, RI: E.L. Freeman and Sons, 1887.

Robinson, Caroline E. *The Gardiners of Narragansett, Being a Genealogy of the Descendants of George Gardiner the Colonist 1638*. Providence, RI, 1919.

Robinson Genealogical and Historical Association. *The Robinsons and Their Kin Folk*. New York: The Association, 1906.

Skinner, Charles M. *Myths and Legends of Our Land*. Philadelphia, PA: J.B. Lippincott Company, 1896.

Smitten, Susan. *Ghost Stories of New England*. Auburn, WA: Ghost House Books, 2003.

Some Account of the Vampires of Onset Past and Present. Boston: S. Woodbury and Company, 1892.

Stevens, Austin N. *Mysterious New England*. Dublin, NH: Yankee Publishers Inc., 1971.

Town of Mattapoisett. *Mattapoisett and Old Rochester, Massachusetts*. New York: Grafton Press, 1907.

Updike, Wilkins. *A History of the Episcopal Church in Narragansett, Rhode Island*. Boston: Merrymount Press, 1907.

Verde, Thomas A. *Maine Ghosts & Legends*. Camden, ME: Down East Books, 1989.

The Vermont Register and Almanac for the Year of Our Lord 1822: Being the Second after Bissextile, or Leap Year and (till July 4) the 46[h] of American Independence. Burlington, VT: E. and T. Mills, 1822.

Walmsley, Amasa E. *Life and Confession of Amasa E. Walmsley*. Providence, RI, 1832.

Walton's Vermont Register and Farmer's Almanac for the Year of Our Lord 1831: Being Third Year after Bissextile or Leap Year and Fifty-fifth of American Independence. Montpelier, VT: E.P. Walton and Co., 1831.

OTHER RESOURCES

Abandoned Rails. www.abandonedrails.com.
The Kennebunk Inn. www.thekennebunkinn.com.
New England Antiquities Research Association. www.neara.org.
New England Families. www.nefamilies.com.
Portsmouth Black Heritage Trail. www.pbhtrail.org.
Quahog. www.quahog.org.
Rhode Island Cemeteries Database. http://ricemeteries.tripod.com.
Rutland, Massachusetts Historical Society. www.rutlandhistoricalsociety.org.
Sam's Good News. www.samsgoodnews.com.
Wikipedia, the Free Encyclopedia. www.wikipedia.org.
Witchcraft and Witches. www.witchcraftandwitches.com.

About the Authors

With thirty-one years experience and more than one thousand investigations, it is no wonder that Tom D'Agostino and Arlene Nicholson have appeared on numerous radio and television shows and documentaries, including A&E Biography Channel's *My Ghost Story*, WGBY's *Things That Go Bump in the Night* ("Tales of Haunted New England," the PBS Documentary series *Haunted Rhode Island* and Animal Planet's *The Haunted*, as well as several appearances on *Ghosts 'R' Near, 30 Odd Minutes* and *Ghost Chronicles* to name a few.

As authors of nine books sold worldwide (*Haunted Rhode Island, Haunted New Hampshire, Haunted Massachusetts, Pirate Ghosts and Phantom Ships, Abandoned Villages and Ghost Towns of New England, A Guide to Haunted New England, A History of Vampires in New England, Haunted Vermont* and *Ghost Stories and Legends of Connecticut*), Tom and Arlene have experienced, recorded, photographed and penned the most incredible haunts and legends the region has to offer while becoming among the most prolific and knowledgeable individuals on the subject of ghosts, legends and folklore.

Their paranormal experiences and stories have appeared in countless publications worldwide. Tom and Arlene are also the organizers of Paranormal United Research Society. They are well respected and celebrated for their years of experience and knowledge in the field of the paranormal.